the WASHETERIA MYSTERY

Who Killed Ruby?

CATHERINE RATHE

Illustrations by – Aryanna Rathe, Claire Rathe and Catherine Rathe

Publishing Coordinator – Sharon Kizziah-Holmes

Paperback-Press
an imprint of A & S Publishing
Paperback Press, LLC
Springfield, Missouri

ISBN -13: 978-1-960499-91-2

DEDICATION

To my loving family whose support and encouragement has been my greatest source of strength throughout this journey. Without you cheering me on every step of the way this project would not have been possible. To my Grandma Helen and Granddad Raymond who are now with the angels, thank you for teaching me so much of what I know. May this tale reach you.

CONTENTS

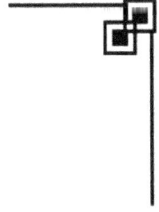

~ PROLOGUE ~

Daily Citizen Oct 1963
MISSING TEACHER

The tragic story of my aunt Ruby's unsolved murder has been part of my life for as long as I can remember. Many stories are often passed down to the next generation, and this story rolled through my generation as smoothly as the wind whipping through the cornfields near my childhood home in Nebraska. The trail of sadness this crime has left behind is beyond expression.

I don't recall any one moment of being told this sordid tale; it's always been hidden away in my mind, silently contributing to what makes me who I am. Ruby had been gone fifteen years when my life began but even through that expanse in time, I feel connected to her and her story. Ruby was, formally speaking, my great, great aunt on my mother's side. Her case has remained unsolved for sixty plus years. To have a loved one murdered so tragically is hard enough, but then you add insult to injury by not receiving any answers or explanation. It makes the aftermath much harder to cope with.

I carried this puzzling mystery with me through childhood, and now it haunts me in adulthood. I have always been intrigued by Ruby's story, and growing up, I wanted to know as much as I could.

I may have driven my mother and grandmother a bit crazy with the number of times I implored, "Now tell me again *exactly* what happened and who you think did it." The times I snuck back to my grandma's office (the restricted part of the house no man shall enter) to catch a glimpse of the Daily Citizen newspaper article about Ruby stowed away, and all the times I made my mother tell and retell the sordid details, are too many to count. And is it just me or does every grandma have a room in their house that is seemingly off limits? For my grandma it was her "office." Always one to push the limits, I would quietly open the door to the forbidden room hoping I wouldn't get caught. Sometimes feeling brave, I would call over my shoulder, in the sweetest voice I could muster, "Grandma? Can you show me the Aunt Ruby article again?" My grandma could usually be found in the kitchen making me something scrumptious to eat or sitting on her sofa stringing green beans from her large garden into an oversized paper bag. In later years, she became a permanent fixture at the head of her exorbitant dining room table, proof reading recipes for a bit of income. I know not a day went by that my grandma didn't think of Aunt Ruby.

One such day of me begging to talk about Aunt Ruby, I received a priceless gift. I called out to my grandma to show me the article once more, and a moment later I heard the creak of the table where she sat stationed. She leaned on the massive structure to lift herself out of her chair and, dutifully but slowly, went to fetch the worn article about Aunt Ruby's murder. This reminds me of a time much later, when I was grown and brought my own children to visit my grandmother. My son Samuel, very young at the time, would say, "Hurry Grandma, run!" as she puttered from counter to table, fixing food for my children. Grandma would reply with a chuckle in her throat, "I don't run, I hobble!" A fond memory.

As my grandma "hobbled" to the office that day long ago, I stood at the door peeking in, hoping to get a better view of all the hordes of items stacked everywhere. Sometimes I would be courageous enough to tiptoe through the narrow, 3-foot path cleared to the closet and quietly slide the door open, my eyes not seeing anything but everything at the same time.

In the cluttered closet, stacks of old paperwork teetered alongside tangled cords and cables, while books and obsolete gadgets gathered dust on sagging shelves. Half empty boxes of stationary mingled with forgotten office supplies, and a mishmash of random items like a broken stapler, faded Bible stickers (rewards for her long reigning bible class my grandma faithfully taught every week), and a box of trinkets from a special trip to Hawaii years ago, crowded the space, creating a chaotic jumble of forgotten belongings waiting to be rediscovered. Then there were the piles of pictures, collections of hair (yes, hair was snipped and kept in remembrance of loved ones), pin cushions, piles of thread for embroidery, and other sewing supplies stacked in organized chaos on the office desk. Years later I found a more impressive item in the depths of her closet. As the family gathered in 2012 to mourn my grandma's passing, my curious nature got the best of me again. I decided to "innocently" scan the closets one more time for old times' sake, and lo and behold…I located my grandma's living will and testimony. A plastic carrying file case perched on top of a pile of miscellaneous items, haphazardly tilted to one side, caught my eye. The contents revealed my dear grandma's final wishes. I smiled and simply whispered in awe, "The Will." I thought it humorous at the time I was the one to unearth this document.

Rewind back to the day when my grandma was fetching the sacred artifact about Aunt Ruby for me once more. Much to my surprise, my grandma handed me the creased, yellowed write up and said, "Here, why don't you just take it with you." This news article was a prized possession that I, being 13, thought would be perfect to keep rolled up in a small film container. I kept Ruby's article safe within the confines of the black and gray tube, along with other special knickknacks, in a bulky old camera case.

I think back to that memory as the upbeat sounds are blaring from my stereo system, current day, in the family SUV. They are distracting to me as my daughter is trying to engage me in light conversation. Sometimes I feel like it's a cinematic experience inside the confines of my SUV, but I can't complain. This mama likes to have her music. The distraction that day was not due to the volume of the song; it was the song itself. The band Kaiser Chiefs was blasting out "Ruby Ruby Rubyyy." I interrupted my daughter mid-sentence and exclaimed, "This song! Did you choose this on purpose?" My daughter knew I had been putting in long hours researching and writing about Ruby's case. My daughter laughed and said, "No I just like this song." I had to gather my thoughts because the number of coincidences that had occurred since I started my latest venture of researching Ruby's case was rattling me a bit. Every time I turned around there were signs, some subtle and some glaring, reminding me of the work I was doing. I started my truth-seeking investigation into my aunt's unsolved murder in early 2022, hoping to share my findings while bringing light to this cold, dark case.

As I would pour over the aged article on Ruby, so many questions came to mind. What happened to this dark haired, almost black-eyed woman, smiling curtly up at me from the tattered newspaper. Did she know her killer? Did the police interview her killer? Is the killer still alive? One can only learn so much from a short newspaper article and idle talk from family. After years of wondering, I decided I needed to know more than what I could learn from family about Aunt Ruby. My mother had previously told me a relative had fought for Ruby's sealed records and won against the Arkansas State Police. The family member had tried to obtain Ruby's records and the request was denied, stating it was an ongoing investigation. The family was quick to say, prove it. If the Arkansas State Police could show they had worked on it in the last few years, that would be an understandable reason for denial. Long story short, they couldn't prove it and the Arkansas Supreme Court sided with the family. Knowing that information made me wonder if I too could have access to Ruby's files. I did some digging and found I could easily request the records through the Freedom of Information Act (FOIA). I did just that. I requested her case load through FOIA and received them rather quickly in April of 2022. As I sifted through her files and contemplated what to include, I knew I wanted to present the facts of the case as delicately as I could. Some of the statements from individuals are hard to digest.

When I received the files through FOIA they were out of order and very hard to read. Hard emotionally and hard technically. Emotionally because this crime touches me to my very soul, and technically because I am not tech savvy. The files were faded, and many were illegible. I slow peddled my way throughout the better part of a year, trying different ways to edit the files to make the words clear. It was an arduous process. When I say blood, sweat, and tears went into this endeavor that is not an exaggeration. At times I would give up and shut my laptop in frustration. But just like when my daughter randomly chose the song "Ruby," there were many other pesky, strange happenings forcing me back on my quest.

One of these nights I had given up on editing the documents and decided to unwind with a tv show. It was a mystery, of course, and the main character finds out the name of the victim was an alias all along. Can you guess what the victim's real name was? The actress clutches the newly found birth certificate as she whispers, "Ruby?? Your real name was Ruby!" And then the actress cries out in frustration, "Oh Ruby what happened to you?" I could relate to the actress's angst, and goosebumps ensued. I've never been one to believe in the supernatural in the way of ghosts, but I may have slept with a nightlight on that night.

To shed light and truth on this puzzling case, I am going to do my best to share what I think would be helpful. I do have a strong sense of duty to present all the facts and allow the reader to be informed and will be including many full statements and polygraph reports at the end of this book. I was correct in thinking there might be more information in the files than was told to family. The worn, faded records uncovered more than I imagined about Ruby's husband, charismatic Doc Stapleton, a lot more. Digging deeper through the files made me want to take this journey wherever it would take me. I started down the path of podcasts, YouTube channels, and super sleuthing.

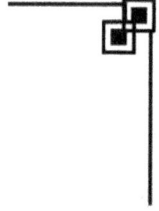

~ CHAPTER ONE ~

Washed in Mystery

On a balmy October night in 1963, police descended on the Norge Launderama in the small town of Searcy, Arkansas. Officers Dean Hunter and Adam Woodruff were met with an ominous scene. The time was approximately midnight. The washeteria was eerily vacant, with someone's items strangely appearing to be abandoned mid wash. Dryers filled with wet clothes, doors ajar, and coins resting in the slots of unstarted machines gave officers a peculiar feeling down their spines.

A basket of freshly dried clothes placed on the floor and a half-used bottle of Wisk laundry soap sitting atop a counter were items also abandoned. A woman was seen washing her clothes earlier that night but had seemingly vanished abruptly, leaving no clues as to where she could be. It was as if someone pushed pause on this moment in time.

The Norge Launderama sat on the outskirts of town on the corner of Main and Lincoln. Nestled in between Harrisons Super Market (later known as Angel's) and Adams Pest Control, the washeteria was like any other laundromat and considered safe. (Adams Pest control is now located across the street from its original location.) People often chose this location to get their loads done quicker. The no frills establishment boasted of quick drying machines and shorter wash times. It wasn't unusual for customers to leave their loads after starting the drying cycle. There was a general comfortableness about retrieving it after work or after running errands. It was unusual though at this late hour for damp clothes to be left to sit, especially in this region of extreme humidity.

The police were conducting a welfare check on fifty-nine-year-old Professor Ruby Stapleton, a resident of Searcy, AR. Well known to her community, Ruby was employed by the English department through the nearby Harding College. Police were contacted by Ruby's twenty-year-old daughter, Mary Claire Stapleton, when her mother was gone much longer than would be expected to launder clothes. The police headed to the washeteria where they experienced the chilling findings. Ruby's things left unattended, and her empty car parked outside, made for suspicious circumstances.

The police were right in thinking this was alarming, and a few days later their suspicions were confirmed when a squirrel hunter stumbled upon Ruby's lifeless body in a dry creek bed 15 miles from the washeteria. Ruby had no known enemies, and with no obvious motive, one could quickly assume the older woman was the victim of a crime of opportunity. Being alone in a washeteria late at night, the surrounding streets dark, as all other businesses were closed, could have created a perfect setting for a random crime. But there were twists and turns that kept investigators guessing and unable to deem this as a wrong place wrong time situation. A crime like this was unusual for the small town of Searcy and even more unusual for whom this crime happened to.

Ruby Was and Searcy Is

Frances Ruby Lowery was born on February 27, 1904, the third of six children born to Benjamin Franklin Lowery and Clara Isabelle Lowery. Ruby was an olive complexioned beauty, with jet black hair and the darkest of brown eyes. Ruby wore her hair braided, her braids expertly woven around her crown, or pinned back in a low chignon. The epitome of a modest woman, Ruby paid little attention to her dress, instead giving attention to her faith, studies, cooking, and family. Ruby, along with her four sisters and one brother, were raised in the small farming community of Davenport, Nebraska. Her sibling's names were Nellie Ruth (my great grandma), Rose Marie, Inez Lillian, Joseph Franklin, and Clara Florence. I find their names to be quite beautiful, and it interests me that all her siblings were called by their middle names, not their chosen first names. I remember visiting my Aunt Lilian in Davenport, Nebraska and never knew her first name was Inez until my research. If my grandma were alive today and reading this, she would correct me and tell me in an exasperated tone, "You did know all of their first names, but you must have forgotten." My grandma Helen was a master historian and info sharer. Brings a smile to my face as I type this. So, Grandma, if you are reading this from heaven, I'll admit I am sure you told me their names, and I forgot.

Growing up among the cornfields of Nebraska, Ruby had a simple, happy upbringing. Dutifully attending church services every week, she listened to her father preach the bible. Ruby's father was also editor of the local newspaper and her mother, a teacher.

Ruby followed in her mother's footsteps and received her degree in teaching. She received her degree from Harding college, now known as Harding University. She began student teaching math in 1925 while finishing her degree. A very small college at the time, Ruby was the only one of her graduating class in 1926. She writes alongside her picture as her quote in a 1925 yearbook, "I'll do that next summer," posing with a coy smile. But knowing what I have heard about Ruby, she certainly was one to do things in a rather timely fashion. She was nicknamed Flutter by her high school classmates and received the title of all-around girl in her early years at college.

Ruby's roots ran deep to her alma mater. Her father, Benjamin Franklin Lowery, helped with the organizing of the college in 1924 before becoming the business manager from 1927-1929 and was on the board of trustees for many years. My parents, grandparents, and many family members have attended Harding from the 1930's, and even up until now the family line continues with cousins at Harding. The Harding campus was originally located in Morrilton, AR and moved to Searcy in 1934. Ruby was put in charge of coordinating the move. The first to help with behind-the-scenes work, she moved many items, deep cleaned buildings, and prepared meals for people aiding in the move. She was key in getting the printing press on the new campus. At night, she would ease out of the long, humid workdays by playing piano with others singing along.

In 1935 she married Ray Stapleton, and they later had two children: a son, Glen Dewey, and then a daughter, Mary Claire. After receiving her master's degree in English and moving around some with her husband, she began teaching at Harding again in 1940. Ray Stapleton was a professor of business at Harding as well, teaching from 1932-1935 and then again from 1940-1953. Ray and Ruby were a crucial part of Harding's formative years, contributing much effort and value to the classes and overall purpose of the college.

◈◈

At age 59, Ruby was hard working, driven, and likable. She was a go getter that got any job done quickly and efficiently. Ruby's parents had relocated to Missouri in 1935 with her father moving closer to Ruby in 1945 after the death of her mother. When Ruby's father fell ill, he moved in with Ruby. Taking on the role of care giver, she cared for him until he passed away in 1955 at her home in Searcy, AR. Ruby was always one to provide instruction and care, and was the ever-doting grandmother. Ruby was accustomed to serving and leading, being heavily involved in various clubs and family relationships.

While not divorced, Ruby and her husband had been living in separate locations for 9 years. Ray Stapleton had taken a job out of state, for reasons known only to a select few, and Ruby had begun managing the household on her own. If there was a leaky pipe under the house, she didn't think twice about crawling under her house, wearing a dress or not, to patch it up. She would take care of the problem, dust off her skirt, and go about her day.

Living through the Great Depression had taught Ruby how to be frugal. If there was a bit of green on the family's bologna, no bother, she would just cut that part off. The refrigerator at the Stapleton house was never empty, always overflowing with leftover food that would remain until eaten.

I remember my grandma having a similar perspective on leftovers. She was skilled at making the most of every meal, never letting any morsel go to waste. Somehow, whatever delicacy she was trying to save made its way into the fridge. I could never understand how she managed to fit one more item in the overstuffed fridge. It was as if a small space would magically open amongst the thousands of items piled inside.

Ruby had the same mindset of frugality when it came to primping. Not giving much time to the latest trends and fashion, Ruby dressed modestly, but according to pictures, her hair was always neatly done. Although she was frugal and simple, she still took the time and means to care for her children's and even student's wellbeing. To say she was zealous for her college and church would be an understatement. Her passions were her family, career, and Christianity. Her life reflected as such.

Ruby's portrait hangs in memory today at Harding's Brackett Library on campus. At times I would visit the library and scour the walls for her portrait. When I would finally locate its resting spot, I would stare up at the painting in thoughtful contemplation. Who would want to hurt this hardworking, kind, Christian Woman?

A bit about Harding

Harding University is a Christian college, with roughly 5,000 students as of 2023. Harding was founded in 1924 in Morrilton, Arkansas, and was launched on biblical principles and offered an education rooted in Christianity. The chosen name Harding was a tribute to James Harding, a student and minister of the church of Christ. John Armstrong was the first president. After the college relocated to Searcy, Dr. George S. Benson became president in 1936, and his tenure lased a long 29 years (he was the president at the time of Ruby's disappearance and had a very close relationship with her).

Provided below is a portion of Harding University's Spiritual Vision as stated on their current website:

Because "God shows no partiality," Harding University is committed to welcoming, accepting, respecting and loving students of every race and nationality. We stand opposed to racism in all of its insidious forms, and we require that everyone who walks on our campus be treated with the dignity and value that everyone deserves by virtue of being an image bearer of God. Harding has always been deeply connected to churches of Christ. Though we live in a time of significant differences among our convictions, we are determined that Harding University will become captive to neither a rigid legalism on the right nor a formless liberalism on the left. "With gentleness and respect," we hold to such distinctive practices as the teaching of baptism for the remission of sins and a cappella music and male spiritual leadership in public worship. While we maintain our close ties with churches of Christ, Harding opens her arms to all. We welcome those who do not share our convictions, as we work tirelessly to offer an exemplary liberal arts education in an environment of kindness, fairness, respect and love.

You may have heard of Harding University through the media in recent years. A tragedy that stole the life of Botham S. Jean has somewhat highlighted Harding University in the news. Botham Jean was a Harding Alumni who was tragically shot and killed by off duty officer Amber Guyger on September 6th, 2018, in Dallas, Texas. She claims she entered Botham's unlocked apartment, incorrectly thinking it was her own apartment. Upon entering, she states that she thought he was an intruder and proceeded to shoot him. Amber Guyger was convicted of murder and sentenced to 10 years.

A group of Harding alumni came together and petitioned to make a change to a prominent building on Harding campus. The group wanted to change the name of the George S. Benson Auditorium to the Botham S. Jean auditorium. Because Botham Jean was a man of color, they sighted Benson's former position on desegregation as a reason to replace Benson's name. In 1956, Benson gave speeches opposing desegregation and was very adamant about keeping Harding free from people of color. The president of Harding University at the time, Bruce McLarty, responded to the request for a name change with a lengthy statement. Included below is a portion of the Harding Bison article from September 4th, 2022, detailing his response. The full article is available at:

https://scholarworks.harding.edu/cgi/viewcontent.cgi?article=29

90&context=thebison

"The name of George S. Benson will remain on the auditorium that now bears his name," McLarty said. "Rather than remove his name, the university needs to tell the more complete story of Dr. Benson – both the high points and the low points, the inspiring and the painful. ... We need to tell the larger, complicated, multifaceted story of this national icon that the Harding family knows as 'Dr. Benson.'"

The article concluded with:

Although the meeting between McLarty and House did not result in a name change, McLarty acknowledged that "we recognized a major oversight as a result of the recent discussions." "Today, we are embarrassed that African Americans were not welcomed as students at Harding until 1963," he said. "I confess to now being embarrassed that even though African Americans have been an important part of the Harding community since 1963, there are no buildings or landmarks that celebrate any of those alumni who have made such a contribution to our university family."

As a response, McLarty announced the organization of a task force that will include black board members, employees, alumni and students whose goal will be to address the challenge of identifying the most meaningful and appropriate ways Harding can celebrate black students at the university. He also still plans on honoring Jean in "some physical way."

"Botham will be honored in his own unique way on our campus," McLarty said. "This could be with a bronze statue of Botham leading singing, or it could be the naming of an academic program in his honor. That remains to be determined, but the name of Botham Jean will be prominently and permanently placed on the Harding campus during the coming school year."

Essentially, the Benson Auditorium would remain under its name to continue honoring George S. Benson, Harding's longest reigning president. After the petition failed to produce the name change, the University opted to create a memorial for Botham S. Jean. The University dedicated his memorial on September 29th, 2021. Botham would have turned 30 on that day. The memorial sits out front of the David B. Burks American Heritage Building and bears Botham's image. The memorial provides a place for students and others to sit and visit or have a quiet moment. There is hope that this memorial will honor Botham's legacy of joy and community that he stood so firmly for.

◈◈

In the fall of 1963, students at Harding College were deep in their studies, preparing for upcoming exams. Awaiting the unbearable heat of summer to give way to the welcomed, cooler temperatures of fall, the campus was alive with activity. No one could have prepared for the event lurking around the corner, causing all activity to cease and lives to be thrown into upheaval.

The distinct fashion of the era was evident throughout campus. The girls, with their A-line skirts, cardigans, and square toed heels, painstakingly rolling their hair every night to hold the neat voluminous style the next day, and the boys, clean shaven with neatly trimmed hair, dressed in sport coats, skinny ties, and matching oxfords, made up the student body at the conservative Christian college.

Many students were preparing that fall for the upcoming yearly retreat at Camp Tekodah. The Harding Chorus was busy practicing for their role in leading the acapella singing at the retreat. Excited young ladies were chosen for the Harding Cheerleading team, and the fifty-member Harding band was proudly preparing for their first debut at a home football game. While enjoying a milkshake at the local snack shack, the Frosty Treat, "Home of the Heavenly Hamburgers," one could most likely hear the Ronettes belting out their number one song of that year, "Be My Baby." With their beehive hair paving the way to newer, fresher hairstyles, the Ronettes were a sight to see and hear. The hairstyles weren't quite that fashion forward on campus. Far past the carrier pigeon era, yet far from the Silicon Valley era, the nation was slowly advancing in fashion and some technology. The students were presented with shiny plastic id cards for the first time.

Advancement in technology wasn't the only change Harding witnessed in 1963. As stated before, Dr. Benson, President of Harding College, once known for his speeches opposing desegregation, ultimately accepted desegregation, admitting the first 3 people of color into Harding college in 1963. Things were changing, and life was going on per usual for the close-knit Harding faculty and student body. Ruby, the dependable, quiet professor was a constant in the students' lives, and the last person anyone would think such a crime could happen to.

The campus was still reeling from their professor's untimely death when one month later, another tragedy struck not just the Harding community but the nation. President John F. Kennedy was gunned down in his motorcade as he traveled through Dealey Plaza in downtown Dallas. Another event that sent shockwaves through the campus. I have pondered what affect, if any, the assassination of the president had on the investigation of Ruby's murder. Did the investigation become stagnant while the nation was consumed with fear and shock as they tried to process the assassination? The Harding community was dealt some heavy blows the fall of 1963.

Searcy is...

Searcy, Arkansas is a sleepy little town of 24,000 residents and rarely makes the headlines. With its respectful yes ma'ams and no ma'ams, the residents don't stir up a lot of controversy. Searcy is forty-four miles northeast from its capitol, Little Rock, and ninety-five miles west of Memphis, Tennessee. Known for the location of Harding University, Searcy boasts a peaceful atmosphere. Harding University being situated in the heart of the town brings jobs and new people every year to the small, close-knit community. People know each other by name and enjoy a slower paced life, focusing on traditional values and local customs. Many families have been here for years, sharing stories and anecdotes passed down from one generation to the next.

While there is no shortage of tranquility and good hospitality in this quiet town, things aren't always picture perfect. Years after Ruby's murder, another shocking crime fired up the town once more. You may have heard of the case. Fern Rodgers, wife of Dr. Porter Rodgers Senior, was shot and killed in 1974. The result of a murder for hire plot. The old doc wanted to trade her in for a younger model. The nation watched the scandalous trial as it played out in news footage and magazine articles. Dr. Rodgers, the hired man, and the mistress were all tried and found guilty in one way or another. Another tragedy and social earthquake for this unassuming town.

Before this tragedy, my mother and Fern crossed paths one afternoon when my mother was a young, college bound 18-year-old. She inquired about renting a room above the Rodgers home in the summer of '74. Fern, being the well-mannered aristocrat she was, offered my mother a cup of tea, and they discussed the terms of the living arrangement. Fern served tea to my mother, and Fern's sister-in-law, Helen Bratten Cowen, accompanied them. Fern was the epitome of a southern lady, and my mother remembers Fern being "dressed to the nines" and as sweet as sweet can be. She said Fern "dressed to dress," unlike women today, who choose comfort over fashion, preferring the popular athleisure style of clothing. What a different time it was back then. Seems like Ruby and Fern had regality in common. Shortly after the afternoon meeting, my mother's plan changed, and she didn't end up living at the Rodgers home. Two short months later, Fern was gunned down by hired hitman, Berry Kimbrell. A very sad day for many people.

Both Aunt Ruby's and Fern Rodger's crimes were similar in that they were heinous and senseless, but there were also differences between the two. The key difference being Ms. Fern received justice, in the criminal sense, and Aunt Ruby did not.

The Porter Rodgers family were key figures at the Searcy Country Club, and still today the club provides social enjoyment for many. It is a popular hub of the city, filled with golf tournaments, social events, and delicious dinners. If you're one of the special ones to frequent the club, I've heard they will make you a place card, reserving your special spot at the bar. And don't worry, you can always find a seat at the local restaurant, Rock House, if you aren't a member at the club.

Being in the east central part of the state, Searcy is, in my opinion, much too humid for any human to endure. (*The humid air would be another hinderance in the investigation due to the heat inducing rapid decomposition of the body*). I've traveled the warm Florida coast, spent numerous sweaty summers in Georgia, endured the sticky air on the plains of Nebraska and am now fighting the thick humidity in Northwest Arkansas. But nothing comes close to the sweltering heat in Searcy that seems to get hotter each time I visit. I might be somewhat spoiled having lived in New Mexico for 13 years where the threat of humidity is as likely as finding ticks. Another marvelous thing found in Arkansas. Although Searcy is humid, most don't complain much and won't let it spoil their fun. The citizens may not have a Target to stroll through to escape the heat, but they have other means to keep cool on hot summer days. They can stop by the Dairy Queen, formerly known as the Tasty Freeze, or throw their lines in the Little Red River and maybe jump in for a swim if the fish aren't biting.

The small town of Searcy may provide peaceful living, a sense of community, and an overall pleasant place to land, but as we all know, small towns come with big secrets.

~ CHAPTER TWO ~

Soiled Memories

Her Last Day

Tuesday, October 8th, 1963, was a typical day for Ruby. Living by the mindset the early bird catches the worm, Ruby was up most mornings by 5 a.m. On Tuesday morning, she woke early and prepared breakfast for Mary Claire and her niece Clarita, who was staying with her at the time. Mary Claire and Clarita had both recently turned twenty years old. Ruby then set her sights on her flower beds. She was seen working in them around 6:30-7 a.m. and was so diligent in her home making that she was late to an 8 a.m. hair appointment.

Ruby arrived at Louise's Beauty Salon at 8:30, apologizing to the owner, Louise Cannon, saying she had been running late due to conversing with the family painter about touching up her house. Ruby had her hair shampooed, dried, and styled. I find it remarkable for 59 years of age, Ruby had little gray hair. Gone were the braids worn for so long, and in their place was a newer, shorter hairstyle.

She taught her first English class that morning at 9:45 and then went back home to enjoy lunch with her daughter and niece. Over lunch, the girls commented on how nice Ruby's hair looked. That afternoon, the college girls had classes, and Ruby taught her afternoon class, freshman English, which ended at 4:35 p.m. She was seen straightening up her desk around 4:45.

That evening, Ruby puttered around the kitchen making dinner for Mary Claire and Clarita before an anticipated bible study that night. The college girls were attending a devotional at 6:30 with their respective boyfriends and had plans to study after. Saying goodbye to Ruby, they headed to the Bible building on the Harding College campus, just a short walk away from their home at 910 East Center Street.

Ruby left soon after the girls, around 7 p.m., to visit her son Glen Dewey before the fateful trip to the washeteria. Glen Dewey Stapleton, and his wife Patricia Rhodes-Stapleton (Pat for short), lived a few miles down the road at their home in Searcy. On her way to their house, Ruby picked up Pat's younger sister, Charlotte Rhodes, to accompany her to see Glen and Pat's newborn baby. Upon arriving at her son's residence, Ruby discovered his washing machine was clogged. Knowing her son and his wife had two small children, one being an infant, she offered to wash their clothes and return them later that night or the next morning. Charlotte, fourteen years old, recalled her last memory with Ruby and provided police with details of the time leading up to her disappearance. I have a feeling of rushed protectiveness over this young, fourteen-year-old girl, who recalled those last moments with Ruby. She must have been so overwhelmed at the time but gave her statement to police with such calm clarity.

Charlotte stated Mrs. Stapleton picked her up from her residence about 7:30 p.m. Ruby said she had bones to give Charlotte's pet dog but told Charlotte to wait to take them inside until they returned home later. They arrived at Glen Dewey's house at approximately 7:40, where they visit, watch tv, and stand around the washer located under the carport, conversing about it being broken. Ruby then offered to wash their clothes, which Glen Dewey agreed for her to do. Ruby left about 9 p.m. to take Charlotte home. Not long after they left, Ruby questioned Charlotte about laundry detergent. She asked Charlotte if she remembered to put the Wisk in the car.

Charlotte says she didn't remember if it was in the car. Ruby pulled over to the shoulder of the road and looked in the backseat. Seeing nothing, she continued down the road remarking "Tide" will work just as well. As they arrived at Charlotte's residence, Ruby reminded her to take the bones in for her dog and waited for the young girl to turn her garage light on before leaving. Charlotte gave a final wave, unaware it would be their last interaction. Ruby pulled away from Charlotte's home in her white comet station wagon, weaving through the streets she had traveled on for over 30 years.

After making sure Charlotte was safely dropped off, Ruby headed home to grab her own laundry before heading to the local washeteria. The time was approximately 9:00 p.m. She was greeted by her niece, Clarita Bartley, who had just returned home from her evening devotional.

Ruby's twenty-year-old niece had been staying with her while attending Harding College. When Ruby's father passed away, he left an inheritance to his children. Clarita's mother, Clara Lowery Bartley, had asked her sister Ruby to take her inheritance in exchange for her daughters, Clarita and Betty, to live with Ruby while they attended Harding college. Ruby was more than willing to open her home to her nieces. Betty had stayed with Ruby previously, and now it was Clarita's turn to attend college. Ruby arrived home to see Clarita standing in the yard, rinsing off her shoes that had been muddied. Ruby greeted her niece and then walked inside to gather her laundry. It would be the last time Ruby entered her home on Center Street situated next to her beloved alma mater.

Clarita Bartley- Ruby's niece

Clarita was named after her mother, Florence Clara. Clarita means "Little Clara" in Spanish. How special that her mother had chosen the name Clarita as a nod to her own name. I remember my grandma speaking fondly of her cousins, and I remembered Clarita specifically because I thought the name Clarita was beautiful and unique. My mother suggested I speak with Clarita about my aunt Ruby's case, knowing Clarita was living with Ruby at the time. If anyone knew facts about this case, it would be Clarita. I reached out to Clarita in June of 2022, and we had an in-depth phone call regarding Ruby's case. While we both share in the fact our conversation was over something so dreadful, it was still a delightful conversation. There is something about connecting with a family member that is very special, even a distant relative. Clarita shared with me her memories of that long ago tragic night. I was thankful she was willing to share her last memory of Ruby with me. In reading over her official statement at the time of the disappearance, I am impressed at her very keen memory. But then again, how could one forget something so monumental?

Clarita Bartley's thoughts, opinions, and memories as told to me

My boyfriend, Jerry, and I had walked from the library at about 8 p.m. and went around the block, of course just to have a little more time together. I accidentally dropped my wool sweater on the ground in some water due to it having rained or it could have been from the construction going on nearby. The significance of that is, when he got me home, I did not go straight in. Jerry left and I turned on the garden hose to wash the mud and water off my legs and while I was standing there, pulling my skirt up a little bit, getting the muddy water off, I saw a black car drive very slowly by and I thought well you're getting a good look aren't you! Then in a couple minutes the same long black car circled back again driving very slowly. On the other side of campus where the Harding laundry was, some of our friends reported seeing the black car driving on their side. So, what it was doing was... (she paused as if replaying the scene in her mind), *circling the whole campus, and most likely waiting for Ruby to come home. It seems like a professional hit to me, with a big black limousine type car driving around. And them finding Ruby stripped of anything identifying her made it seem like a hit.*

She goes on sharing with me.

Aunt Ruby had new wall to wall carpet put into the living room, so I knew I didn't dare go in that way. I went the back way and went upstairs to try and wash the dirt out of my wool sweater. It shrunk of course to the size a little baby would wear, and at that point Ruby came home and said she had been at her son Glen Dewey's house and was on her way to the washeteria. She asked me if I needed any clothes washed and called up the stairs before leaving, "Do you

want to come along with me to the washeteria?" I said, "No, thank you." I had washed recently and I told her, "See you later, bye."
That was the last time she saw or spoke to Aunt Ruby. Clarita shares with me the lingering questions in her mind: what if she would have accompanied Aunt Ruby to the washeteria? Would Ruby still have gone missing? She was wise in thinking she herself might have been harmed as well, and she also stated the perpetrator eventually might have carried out the crime another night. There are many theories as to the reason for this crime, one theory being: this crime was not random. The circling of the car would lean into that theory.

Clarita then shared more details of her memory of that night. She said many people reported seeing a long black car parked behind Ruby's car at the washeteria. She admits there were several reports, and it was hard to know what was accurate, but the people reporting the car at the laundromat took notice because it was odd that the car was blocking in another car.

The night Ruby went missing, Dr. Benson was informed, and he stopped by Ruby's house to check on Mary Claire and Clarita. He did not want the girls staying alone at the house, so he asked Jerry and his roommate Ralph McCluggage to stay over. Dr. Benson knew the boys were very trustworthy. Ralph was a nephew to Jimmy Allen, a known friend to Dr. Benson. Jimmy Allen was a former student of Harding and had gone on to be a nationally known gospel preacher. Dr. Benson knew the family well. Jerry and Ralph slept in the downstairs bedroom while Mary Claire and Clarita slept upstairs in Clarita's bedroom.

Clarita continued sharing key things with me.

Dr. Benson said, "When Ruby comes home, you'll still need to continue your college and if Ruby never comes home, you'll still need to continue your college. Even if you don't get anything out of it, I want you girls to go to class and learn what you can. Keep your routine as normal as possible and think of your future."

The next day Ray showed up and it wasn't necessary for the boys to stay anymore but Ray really wanted them to. He kept saying what nice boys they were and to stay as long as they wanted. Jerry and Ralph did not stay. Ray slept in Ruby's bedroom.

One day not long before Ruby disappeared, I saw a letter addressed to Ray telling him she had taken him off their checking account. I also noticed in the days before she would stand at a small window next to a large buffet type furniture the phone was resting on and stare out at the street. I don't know what she was afraid of, but I think she knew something was up because of the letter. She had never stood beside that window before looking so depressed and worried. It was so unusual to me, but I was young and in college and there were things happening all around me that I didn't know were important.

The police interviewed me at the police station and when they were dropping me off the policeman said, "Now you be careful in there. We have a list as long as your arm of known Chicago type gangsters that are friends of Ray's."

Maybe Ray didn't want Ruby dead, but he was being beat up a lot by people at different times and maybe he said he couldn't get money because Ruby wasn't letting him have access to it. And maybe they took it upon themselves to come down and kill her. (More on this later in book)

Another thing we all found interesting was that Ruby didn't want wall to wall carpeting. She had many students visiting her and people coming and going. She thought carpet would be too hard to keep clean. In fact, she had a large piano in her home and there had to be boards put under it through the window to hoist it up to put the carpet in. But Ray wanted it even though he lived out of state and Ruby's garage was filled with Ray's things. A stove and other furniture. It seemed like he was planning to come back even though Harding wouldn't let him teach there again. He came back after Ruby disappeared and he moved all his stuff back in the house like it was his now.

I moved into the dorms and Mary Claire came to visit me once. She said Ray told her even if Ruby comes back, they won't let her stay because they are much better off without her. I was shocked that she would say that about her mother, but I knew Ray was brain washing her.

I interrupted and asked if Mary Claire had ever talked about her mother that way before her disappearance. Clarita went on.

They fussed and fought all the time. Mary Claire was my cousin and I sure love her, but she was 20 going on 12. She would pitch fits and scream and slam doors. Ruby would look like a whipped pup. Mary Claire was mad that Ruby set boundaries. That's why I think Mary Claire was an easy target for Ray to manipulate.

One night Ray was outside screaming at some boys from Harding that had beaten the daylights out of him. We didn't know what was going on.

She continued sharing what Ruby was like in her eyes and other things.

Ruby was an amazing woman, and she had a lot of foresight. Ruby could see that the college was going to grow, and she bought four properties across the college over the years knowing they would become valuable to the college. Ruby had her quirks and liked to save money. She often wore a white blouse and black skirt to teach. She also didn't hesitate to take care of matters of the home. She was a do it yourselfer. She would fix whatever needed fixin and wash her hands, dust off her skirt, and run across the street to teach her English class. Ruby was a pack rat. My mama too. And all the sisters. They kept everything. If they had tin foil they would wash and reuse. Jerry and Ralph cleaned out the fridge to make room for food from friends and the stuff in the back of the fridge would have been a great culture study for a science experiment.

Mother and Daddy came to the funeral and her funeral was a closed casket of course. It was October, hot and humid and her hair had fallen from her scalp.

I go into more details on the memories Clarita shared with me later in the book and her full statement is included. Again, I am thankful she shared her thoughts so freely.

10 p.m. on October 8th. 910 Center Street

At the Stapleton residence the clock ticked on. Mary Claire returned home from studying at the library around 10 p.m., and Clarita informed her Ruby was gone washing clothes. The girls chatted in their rooms upstairs for a little while before Mary Claire went downstairs to do some more studying. At 11 p.m., Mary Claire went upstairs to where Clarita was busy rolling her hair for the night. She expressed worry about her mother not being home at the late hour. A short time later, Mary Claire tried to find the number to the Norge Launderama to no avail. At this point, Mary Claire decided to make the call to law enforcement, asking them to check on her mother at the washeteria if they had an officer in the area. The police sent Officer Woodruff and Officer Hunter to the Norge Launderama, and they found Ruby's car with some of her belongings, but no Ruby. Ruby's daughter was contacted and made aware Ruby was not found at the washeteria. Mary Claire then requested a ride from the officer to the washeteria. Officer Woodruff obliged and accompanied Ruby's daughter to the Norge Launderama. Clarita chose to stay back at the residence, locking the door tight, still hopeful for good news on her aunt's whereabouts.

The duo arrived at the washeteria and upon seeing for herself her mother was not there, Mary Claire asked the officer to take her to Glen Dewey's house immediately. The policeman and Mary Claire made the 5-minute drive to her brother's house. When they arrived, it took persistent knocking and a few minutes for Glen Dewey to sleepily answer the door. Neither he nor his wife Pat had any idea where Glen's mother could be, stating they hadn't seen Ruby since she left hours earlier, soiled wash in tow. Glen Dewey later gave a statement to police that essentially lined up with Charlotte's account of their time at Glen Dewey's earlier.

The officer left Mary Claire at her brother's house, and the siblings decided to head to the washeteria again. They decided it would be best to leave the children with family while they had a second look. Glen Dewey, Mary Claire, and Pat loaded up their two-and-a-half-year-old son and infant son. They took the older child to Pats mothers' home (fourteen-year-old Charlotte's residence) and dropped off the infant with Clarita at Ruby's home. The desperate search for the missing professor was underway. The police spoke to bystanders and wrote up a timeline of Ruby's activity that night at the Norge Launderama.

Police file
Evidence at Scene: Abduction: Facts

The victim entered the structure and placed her soiled clothing contained in baskets on the floor. She engaged the attendant Mrs. C.R. Reggie, in brief conversation, then walked next door to Harrison's Grocery, where she purchased a container of Wisk and promptly returned to the Launderama. The victim then began to wash her clothing and was so engaged when the attendant and her husband, an employee of Harrison's grocery, closed the grocery and left the victim in the Launderama alone at 10:10 p.m. James William, operator of the Seurcy Roller rink, closed his business at 10:00 p.m. October 8th, 1963, and left the rink about 10:30 p.m. He drove the three miles distance to the area of abduction and as he passed the Norge Launderama between 10:30 and 10:40 p.m. he observed an unidentified woman alone in the Launderama apparently engaged in washing clothing. Jack Gardner, employee of Porter Rodgers Farms, had washed his clothing earlier in the day of October 8th and left the clothing at the laundromat. At 10:55 p.m. on the same date, Gardner returned to the laundromat to pick up his clothing. He observed a white comet station wagon parked in front of the building and noticed a basket of clothing which appeared to have been a completed wash on the floor of the Launderama and in front of a dryer. He also noticed the door of this dryer was open and it was partially filled with clothing. He observed no person in or around the launderama.

End of police note on abduction: Facts

This timeline gives a clear indication of when the abduction most likely occurred. According to these records, we can assume after some mundane small talk, Ruby set to work on washing her clothes around 9:30 p.m. Since Ruby was seen washing her clothes by James William around 10:30, we can determine shortly before Jack Gardner returned to collect his wash, between 10:40 p.m. and 10:55 p.m., Ruby encountered the perpetrator or perpetrators and vanished. I often wonder and try not to think about what was going through Ruby's mind as she met with the horrifying circumstance. I believe she was rightfully fearful and possibly even predicted her untimely fate.

On their way back to the washeteria, the police notified the sheriff and conducted a more thorough search of the premises when they arrived. When Officer Woodruff initially searched the area, he discovered a minor break in at the Brookshire Tire Shop. Upon further investigation, the police found not one, but two tire shops had been broken into. Perhaps these break ins would lead to a clue in Ruby's disappearance. The City Tire shop and Brookshire Tire shop were located just one-to-two blocks north from the launderama. Was it possible law-abiding Mrs. Stapleton interrupted a robbery and got in over her head, trying to stop the delinquents?

The police weren't so sure. The tire shop entrances were not visible from inside the laundromat, and the thieves didn't get away with much, just about 3 dollars in change.

After discovering Ruby was murdered, it gave the police even more reason to discard the theory about the robberies and kidnapping being connected. The police said it seemed unlikely criminals of this low scale would commit an act so heinous as kidnapping or murder; although, it does seem like an eerie coincidence. The police eventually caught the five young men who robbed the tire stores and hauled them in for questioning. They denied involvement in Mrs. Stapleton's disappearance and agreed to polygraphs. Polygraphs are not admissible in court, and there is much speculation about the validity of these tests, but it needs to be noted: all these youths passed polygraphs. When questioned about harming Ruby or being involved with her abduction, they stated "no," and the answers were marked truthful by the polygrapher. I pondered the idea of an unknown source influencing these unsuspecting youths to commit the crimes near the laundromat where they would be an easy target to implicate in Ruby's disappearance. Purely speculation but one worth considering as every angle should be explored.

Once it was clear Ruby had vanished, calls started, letting family and friends know Ruby had disappeared with no reason as to why. Although Ruby's extended family lived 700 miles away, they were still close as close could be. My mother remembers my grandma receiving an early morning phone call on Wednesday October 9, alerting her to Ruby's disappearance. Ruby's sister was my grandma's mother, Ruth. My own mother, 8 years old at the time, recalls my grandma hysterical with worry. This was so unlike her Aunt Ruby to go missing. They thought of every scenario imaginable. From taking ill, going to the hospital, to going somewhere with family. Even wondering if Ruby got disoriented and tried to make her way back to her parent's former home in Missouri. My Grandma had a desperate thought of driving to the homeplace to search for her mother's beloved sister. It was all anyone could do but wait with worry and pray.

~ CHAPTER THREE ~

Sensing Evil

F ear blanketed the community as the news of Ruby's disappearance settled in around town Wednesday morning. The unknown whereabouts of Professor Ruby Stapleton had everyone's full attention. The campus was filled with eager students wanting to help search. Dr. Benson allowed classes to be cancelled to aid in the search. For two days, citizens of Searcy, five hundred students, numerous faculty members, and even members of the Civil Air Patrol rallied together and searched. The boys helped search while the girls kept prayer vigils. There were so many out searching that the police received calls from fearful residents reporting suspicious people walking around their yards. The police reassured worried callers the people seen walking through yards were volunteers searching. Everyone was looking and praying for the well-known, predictable professor.

During my quest for information on this case, I met with Hannah Wood, the lead archivist of Harding's Brackett Library. She was a vital part of my research in this case, aiding me in my quest for pictures and articles. I am truly grateful for her time and energy. She shared with me an ironic coincidence. Her father was enrolled as a freshman at Harding college when Ruby was murdered. He took part in the searches for Ruby with other Harding students immediately following her disappearance. Ms. Wood shared with me her father's feeling of how traumatic this was for the students at Harding. This crime instilled a new fear in the community and surrounding areas.

Ms. Wood was not the only one that spoke to me about the fear on campus in 1963. A current professor from Harding University, who chooses to remain anonymous, shared an observation between Ruby's case and a current case in the news. She was a young girl at the time, attending the same church as Ruby, when Ruby was killed. She recalled the fear on campus as being extreme. Below is the sharp perception she shared relating to the cases in one of our email exchanges.

I've thought of your research as I've heard the news about the university in Idaho. I think the fear of the town and the university now is similar to the way it was in Searcy and at Harding. I saw an article in either the Bison or the Searcy paper (I think) that described this. I remember it made me feel better to read of the terror others felt who were much older than I.

The article she remembered from 1963 detailed the terror in the hearts and minds of students on campus. The atmosphere of dread on Harding's campus could easily be compared to the horror the students at the University of Idaho felt when 4 college students were tragically murdered on November 13th, 2022. It was comforting to this professor that even the more mature Harding students were just as scared as she was. No matter the age, there was a fear instilled in everyone's hearts.

Police continued their interviews and met with Mary Claire once again. Replaying Ruby's last day in her mind, Mary Claire recalled the same curious observation Clarita noticed about those last moments with her mother. Mary Claire stated she observed her mother standing by a window in her house as she watched the street outside, as if waiting for someone. An excerpt from Mary Claire's statement to police sheds light on Ruby's behavior.

Listed as Supplement #4
Statement from Mary Claire Stapleton on October 14th, 1963

After supper meal, (I was home about 5:30 and Mother was out puttering around. Mother came in and asked Clarita and me what we wanted for supper). It was getting pretty late. About 6:00 p.m. Clarita ate a sandwich, and I told Mother I didn't care what I ate, and I went into the bathroom to fix my hair. And when I came out about 6:15, Mother was standing there with nothing fixed for me to eat. I asked her why she hadn't fixed me something to eat, and she told me she didn't know what I wanted to eat. I told her she could have walked down to the bathroom and asked me. I don't remember that she said anything. I thought at the time this was unusual because she normally fixed me anything she had handy when I told her I didn't care what I ate. She also normally rushed around and fixed me something to eat when I was in a rush for classes or other activities. On this evening when I entered the room, she was simply standing and looking out the window. This is something mother very rarely or never did before. Mother is just like a fire engine going 90 to nothing all the time.

What was occupying Ruby's mind in those moments on her last day alive? Could Ruby have sensed her misfortune? It was known to many a strange incident a month prior shook Ruby up. Two men broke into Ruby's house and were hiding in a closet. She ultimately got away by means of a rolling pin or something similar she had grabbed and waved at the men. She ran to the nearby campus, and the men were never caught or identified. Not much is known on that occurrence. Who were the men? Was it a coincidence Ruby suffered a break in and shortly after, met her demise?

Another suspicious incident was also reported, coincidently by a current family friend, right after the disappearance. He is older in years, but still remembers the strange account of what he saw. He was a young medical student attending Harding at the time, living near Ruby's house on Center Street. He observed a dark colored sedan parked with its lights off, idling behind Ruby's house, in the days leading up to her disappearance. He thought it was strange and when he heard of Ruby's disappearance, it raised more suspicions in his mind. He wondered why a car was parked in such a way, as if to be spying on Ruby's home. This man also recalled a few young men conversing behind Ruby's house with Doc Stapleton at different times after the crime, and he considered it a bit peculiar. He pondered as to why the group was gathered there. We will likely never know what the reason was. We also will likely never know if the men hiding in Ruby's closet or if the idling car had any ties to her murder.

Another giant question mark lingering in this mystery is that of the letters Clarita mentioned to me and law enforcement. Clarita relayed to me that during the days after Ruby's disappearance, she remembered something Ruby shared with her. While living with her aunt Ruby, Clarita grew quite close with her, and Ruby would confide in Clarita about personal things. Ruby told Clarita she received a letter from her husband Ray, and it caused Ruby to feel upset. Clarita didn't know the contents of the letter but knew it was threatening in some way, and Ruby was concerned. She pondered if this letter was the cause for Ruby's behavior on that last day.

Clarita also shared with me she stumbled upon a different letter before the crime as well. This other letter is mentioned in Clarita's formal statement. Ruby had penned it herself and could possibly be in response to the threatening letter in question. It was written a couple of months before Ruby's disappearance.

Ruby kept her kitchen table as an office of sorts, and there were numerous piles of papers stacked around the surfaces in the kitchen. Amid the paperwork was a letter addressed to Ray. Ruby had a habit of keeping a copy of all letters she wrote, and Clarita, ever the curious young lady, glanced over the letter left on the kitchen table. She remembers reading a portion where Ruby stated Ray should, "Go to the F.B.I. These men won't stop until they get what they want." Clarita was unclear of the meaning of this, but certainly Ray had made it known to Ruby someone was bothering him enough for her to tell him to report it to the F.B.I. Other parts of the letter were Ruby pleading with Ray not to go through with a divorce. She told him she would sell her property to Harding College if he didn't go through with the divorce. Clarita relayed this information about the letter she read to police, and in the days after Ruby went missing, an investigator asked Clarita to find the letter if possible. The police were going to bring Ray and Mary Claire to the station for a joint interview to give time for Clarita to go into the home and search for the letter. Clarita thinks now Ray would already have likely found it and destroyed it. But still, Clarita would have looked for the letter back then, but her parents had already moved her into the dorms at Harding.

When Clarita's parents were informed of Ruby's disappearance, much to Clarita's surprise, her father and a friend traveled to Searcy quickly, arriving there on October 10th. Clarita told me, *"When I answered a knock on the door, I was surprised to see father standing there. He tells me he received a call from Dr. Benson advising him to come to Searcy considering Aunt Ruby's disappearance. He then took me outside and stated why he had come so quickly."* The reason being more than just because Aunt Ruby was missing. She explained to me why her father had traveled with urgency to Searcy. Dr Benson's years long, loyal, and perceptive secretary, Marguerite O'Banion, had informed Benson she had a hunch Clarita's parents were unaware of secrets Ray was keeping and thought it would be pertinent to inform them. Ray had an uncommon way of living for 1963 few knew about. Clarita relayed the conversation she was told her father had with Dr. Benson. *"Ms. O'Banion did not think Mother and Daddy knew about Uncle Ray's secrets and advised it would be wise to fill them in. He called my father,* (shared the well-kept secret), *and my father made the drive to Searcy immediately."* Apparently, Ray coming back to Searcy, while the search for Ruby was taking place, caused Clarita's father to act in haste to retrieve his daughter. The secret revealed was a bombshell to Clarita and her parents. When she told her father that she was asked to search for the letter, her father stated in no uncertain terms, "You are not to go into that house. Leave the detective work to the detectives."

I am unaware if the letter in question was ever found, and I did not come across it in the FOIA files. Was Ray involved in something that caused Ruby to become a target? Could the letter have been a clue to Ruby's demise?

Another strange observation on the day of Ruby's kidnapping was made from a friend of Mary Claire's. Deanna Mills Brooks was with her grandfather when they saw Ruby pull up across from them at a four-way stop. They noticed she was visibly upset and tried to get her attention, but Ruby didn't respond. Deanna's grandfather remarked, "She's angry about something. Something has happened." The cause of her agitation might have been rumors swirling around that a bootlegger was selling liquor to Harding students.

Among the many theories as to why this crime happened, was the theory that Ruby was doing her own investigation on a bootlegging ring going on in Searcy and was silenced. Ruby had a deep sense of good in her inmost being, wanting to stray from wild living, as some would call it, and uphold the values found in the bible. She was concerned about Harding students gaining access to liquor. Was she silenced as to not expose who could be aiding in the illegal action?

❖

A relative of mine shared with me another bit of curious evidence adding more questions to this intriguing case. It could be a completely unimportant piece of information just adding to the many confusing aspects of this case, but I want to include it nonetheless. At some point after Ruby's murder, a strange discovery was made in Ruby's belongings and may or may not have significance in her disappearance. Curiously found in her home among her papers were discarded receipts or "trash" from Dr. Porter Rodgers' residence. Yes, the same doctor who hired someone to kill his wife, Fern.

There is much mystery surrounding this claim. No one has been able to understand why the trash was there in her possession. The implication was that Ruby retrieved the trash/receipts discreetly somehow, as though searching for something. Was she suspecting Dr. Rodgers of contributing to the crime of bootlegging? Did Ruby suspect Dr. Rodgers of something else she had kept to herself? Was the trash wrongly delivered mail, being deposited to Ruby's residence by mistake, or was it actual mail plucked out of the Rodgers' trash by Ruby for some reason? It would seem unlikely for receipts to mistakenly make their way over to Ruby's residence but not impossible. Sadly, I don't think we will ever get answers to these questions.

Growing up I can remember hearing this information and creating a scenario in my head. It played out in my mind like a scene from a movie. I would imagine my aunt Ruby stealthily creeping down an alley after dark, to a dumpster behind Porter Rodgers house, carefully lifting the lid and searching for any evidence of wrongdoing as it would relate to illicit liquor. Years before the mansion was torn down, I was able to visit the infamous doctors house and recall thinking it had the perfect, somewhat hidden type of alleyway for a determined do-gooder to sneak around undetected. An obvious landmark for the town of Searcy, Dr. Porter Rodgers' stately home was situated on the corner of Race Street and North Oak, a few blocks west from Ruby's home on Center Street. It had a large lot with the backyard leading out to a somewhat secluded back street. In my child-like mind, I had constructed a plausible lead. Now as an adult I recognize the unlikeliness of this scenario, but when you are young, it is amazing the places your mind goes.

Even though Dr. Rodgers didn't exactly have a stellar reputation, it does not mean he was involved in what the naysayers were suggesting. Dr. Porter Rodgers was a common name in every household at the time, and many people seemed to love and respect Dr. Rodgers. Although, the town was divided on his expertise in the medical field. Many raved about the doc's wonderful bedside manner and were proud to say he delivered their babies. But then there were those with stories of neglect and harm.

During my frequent inquiries regarding my aunt Ruby's case, I learned of an incident validating the negative reviews the doctor and his hospital received. An employee of a Coke Bottle factory in Searcy suffered a work-related injury. The young man was lifting a giant, heavy, wooden box of Coke bottles, and somehow the box slipped. The glass Coke bottles shattered, and one of the shards caused a significant gnash in his arm. The man was admitted to Porter Rodgers' hospital where they treated and dressed the wound.

With the family at his bedside during his recovery, they began to smell a horrible stench in the air. They realized they hadn't seen the nurses change his dressing in quite some time. After inquiring of the nurses several times to check the bandage without action, they demanded for the nurses to unwrap the bandage. The smell turned out to be anyone's worst nightmare. They found maggots in the wound. Due to the gross negligence of the staff, the nerves had been left so damaged from the severe infection, he was unable to use his hand for the rest of his life. The person who shared this story stated the man's hand remains convulsed in a clenched like state still to this day.

Was Dr. Rodgers an easy person to speculate about because he did have a tainted past? Perhaps that is why mine and other people's minds went to the extreme. Dr. Rodgers was a known gambler and a frequent visitor to casinos in Las Vegas. Rumored to be in deep financial trouble, he was arrested for insurance fraud, and his license to prescribe certain drugs was revoked. And as we know, he was convicted of hiring someone to murder his wife years after Ruby's death, in 1974. In the early 1940's, Dr Rodgers had also been indicted for counterfeit money laundering but subsequently was able to put the charge behind him and continue a successful medical practice until his arrest in 1974. There were rumors about Dr. Rodgers having unscrupulous associations, even some rumors going as far as saying he had ties to the mafia, "La Cosa Nostra."

There were also rumors regarding Ray's criminal ties and possible connections to the mafia in Chicago. Clarita shared with me the curious statement made to her regarding Uncle Ray in the immediate days following Ruby's abduction. She was told Ray's association with "thugs" from Chicago was well known in the small circle of law enforcement in Searcy. Essentially, it was insinuated Clarita should stay clear from Uncle Ray as to not become associated with any such individuals.

Is there significance to this? Is it a coincidence rumors circulating throughout the small town of Searcy were similar regarding Dr. Stapleton and Dr. Rodgers? Is it possible these things were connected in some way? Ruby's death, the trash found in Ruby's home, possible criminal ties between the two? Is there a missing link? It is agonizing not to have any answers to these questions.

Although the negligence story about the factory workers accident is a very serious claim, it does not give reason as to why Ruby had the Doctor's trash in her possession. It certainly does not give motive to a crime. Only motive for mouths to be talking and speculating on the Doctor's reputation, which we all know can only add more mystery and confusion to an already mysterious crime. Again, I am trying to provide all evidence as it was shared with me even if there remain more questions than answers.

A man by the name of Oren Ray Hays (or possibly spelled Oran) also came up in discussions about the bootlegging theory, which seems more plausible than what my childlike mind was dreaming up. He was a known bootlegger and would not want anyone nosing around his unwholesome dealings. Was Ruby getting close to exposing his secret? Could he have done something to Ruby to protect his underground business? Police found nothing to connect him to her case, although tongues were wagging. Some say his car was seen at the washeteria, and he was seen with bloody clothes at the Harding laundromat after Ruby's murder. According to law enforcement at the time, the bloody clothes he allegedly brought into the laundromat were chalked up to have been bloodied from hunting. The details on these accounts are scarce. Not much is documented in the police files I received. I must question why a person, if guilty of murder, would take evidence into a public service place. Stranger things have happened but still, it caused me to question the likelihood of that occurring.

Something of interest happened involving Oren Hays one month after Ruby was killed. Oren Hays' wife died from strychnine poisoning, and he was questioned in her death. But nothing tied him to the murder, and he was never arrested for his wife's death or Ruby's. He had numerous run-ins with the law and was even charged for a myriad of crimes but never was convicted. Some were rumored to believe there was corruption in the sheriff's department and that was the reason Oren Hays kept escaping prosecution.

Could this be part of a larger cover up? The deeper I delved into Ruby's case files, the deeper the mystery seemed to get. So many leads and so many dead ends. All the scenarios were looking to fit the crime perfectly, yet not one was deemed the answer to this mystery.

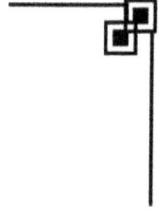

~ CHAPTER FOUR ~

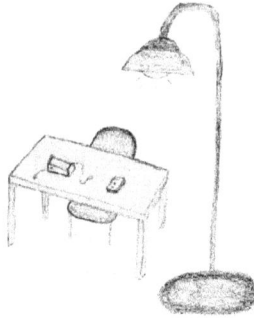

Unfolding Secrets

E mmett Ray Stapleton was born in Hunt County Texas, near Greenville, to James Emmett Stapleton and Mary Elizabeth (Ricketts) Stapleton. Like Ruby's humble upbringing, he grew up in a small farming community. Born on February 5th, 1905, he was younger by almost one year to the day than his wife Ruby. Ray had two siblings. A brother, Willie Garnett, and a sister, Leola G. He finished high school in Wolfe City, Texas and from there attended Harding in the fall of 1926 where he met the raven-haired Ruby Lowery. Graduating with a bachelor's in 1932, Ray later went on to become a professor of business. The two shared their deep love of education, and their Christianity was a bond they shared, at least for a time. After wedding bells chimed for the couple in June of 1935, the Stapletons moved to Alabama. Ruby worked in the school systems, and Ray worked as a treasurer for an apple orchard company. Briefly relocating to Alpine, AR to work in the schools, they headed back to their alma mater where the Stapletons began their tenure in 1940 at Harding College.

Dr. Ray Stapleton was thought of fondly by many. He was known on campus to be quite jovial and liked to 'talk loud,' 'sing loud,' and 'smile loud.' Even today, many people talk of Ray's outgoing personality and remember him as an asset to Harding in general. Dr. Stapleton and Professor Stapleton were a powerful pairing, having strong importance and significance to the college. Both committed to Harding college, they were instrumental in the development and growth of the campus.

Their marriage was one considered to be traditional for the times. Although Ruby was headstrong and independent, in her marriage she remained quietly in the background, while Ray's outgoing and flamboyant personality took center stage. Ruby could hold her own, being sharp as a whip and clever as they come, but she was more inclined to take the role of costar than leading lady. In contrast to her demeanor in marriage, her reputation was a strong leading lady on campus, being involved in leadership roles of various groups and clubs.

Ruby was raised under the guidelines women are to be a "help meet" to the man and marriage is a God ordained covenant relationship. Ruby followed her faith, remaining steadfast in that doctrine: possibly one of the key reasons for not divorcing. Ruby chose to stay by Ray's side even if the marriage was turbulent and even if the marriage covenant was broken.

In 1948, the Harding College Yearbook featured Dr. Ray Stapleton in a full-page dedication reading, *"In tribute to him for his long service and sincere interest in Harding college for his faith in the ability and character of youth, for his enthusiasm and friendliness toward all of us for his faithful Christian life, and the example he has been to us who have known him."* I gasped out loud in utter shock when I came across this tribute, knowing from the information in the police files the college had asked him to resign for reasons that would not be considered honorable according to their beliefs. I wrongly speculated Harding may have dedicated this yearbook as a cover up for the reason he was leaving. I researched it further and learned Ray didn't leave Harding until 1953. So, they may not have known his secret habits at the time of the dedication. Unfortunately, we may never uncover when and who knew of Rays' secrets at the time of his termination.

As mentioned before, Ray and Ruby had been living apart for years, yet remained married. Ray had been moving around the country taking different teaching positions at colleges in the years leading up to Ruby's death. He was never in one place for too long and, in 1963, had just started working at a college in Wisconsin. As such, the police were eager to talk with him.

Dr. Ray Stapleton was notified by his son Glen Dewey of Ruby's disappearance, and Ray quickly left enroute to Arkansas from his home in Superior, Wisconsin. He flew to Memphis and from there traveled to Searcy, arriving on the evening of October 9th. Ray gave the police his first statement a day after arriving in Searcy. The police went about scrutinizing every detail of Ray and Ruby's life in hopes of gaining insight as to why this seemingly simple, law-abiding woman went missing.

Ray's whereabouts were confirmed for the night of October 8th. He was almost 1,000 miles away in Wisconsin, instructing classes at Superior State College late in the day. It would have been physically impossible for Ray to have been anywhere near the washeteria. Unfortunately, Dr. Stapleton claimed he didn't have any idea where his wife could be, but he did give investigators his opinion of who could have taken his wife. I have included a portion below from his initial statement, where he is somewhat positive towards Ruby.

Summary of E.R. Stapleton
Part 1

E.R. Stapleton, husband of the victim, was interviewed in Searcy, AR at 11:00 a.m. October 10th, 1963, and related, that he was then engaged in teaching at Superior State College Superior, WI, where he had been employed since the first week of September 1963. Stapleton continued by stating he had last seen his wife during the last few days of August 1963 at the time of his departure from Searcy, enroute to Superior, WI and he had communicated with her both by phone and letter on two or three occasions after his departure. When questioned about his opinion regarding the victim's disappearance he replied that his only thought was abduction by transients, possibly Mexicans who travel the area between Illinois and Texas. He elaborated on this theory by stating his wife was very dark complexioned and had the appearance of being of Spanish descent. He remarked that his wife had led a golden life, was very dedicated to the church and school, and had constantly worked toward a goal in her life. He denied when questioned that he was separated from his wife due to marital troubles, and quick to express he loved his wife very much. He kept in very close contact with her and the family, and his only reason for working away from home was due to a disagreement with policy at Harding College. Stapleton then remarked he was trying his best to bear up under his wife's disappearance and make the best of the situation because of his daughter's grief. Stapleton states he wants to assure investigators of his complete cooperation in this matter, and at this point in the conversation he began to sob and cry. After the tears were dried away, he made the remark his wife was loved by everyone, and his only complaint ever was, she had lost her sense of values and appeared more dedicated to the church and school than to her home. [End of excerpt.]

This initial interview seems to be unassuming and not overly suspicious. Although, the thought transients preyed on Ruby because of her darker skin tone seems misguided. Perhaps Ray was grasping at straws trying to suggest possible scenarios. Police concluded their interview, and Ray went back to the home on Center Street.

About an hour after Dr. Stapleton's initial interview on October 10th, an intriguing development occurred. The sheriff's office was informed a call had been made to the Stapleton's residence from a person demanding money. The assumption that it was a call from kidnappers was a valid assumption. Ray stayed on the phone for 30 minutes, and police were able to trace the call back to a phone booth outside a drugstore in Lubbock, Texas. The local police in Lubbock were quick to travel to the drugstore and apprehend two men, Gray F. Chandler, and Karl Karash.

The duo gave an interview to the F.B.I. upon being arrested, and the suspected kidnappers were found to be unlikely acquaintances of Ray's. From the very start of the interview, both men denied the allegation they were demanding a ransom relating to Ruby. Karash claimed they called Ray as a friend, who had provided them cash, on many occasions prior. Karash provided the F.B.I. a timeline of sorts to establish an alibi and explained how the duo met Dr. Stapleton. Karash stated while hitchhiking through North Carolina, where Dr. Stapleton had been teaching the previous spring, he was approached by Ray. He said Ray pulled up in his "pink rose Cadillac" and offered him a ride. He accepted the ride and hence started their relationship. Karash went on to tell of his living arrangement and personal details of his life with the professor. Eventually Karash reunited with a former friend, Gray F. Chandler, where Chandler also joined Karash in living with the professor that spring. After they stayed a few weeks in the professor's home they traveled on to Texas, stopping at various locations on the way. They both claimed while traveling from place to place, they received money from Ray multiple times.

Karash and Chandler arrived in Lubbock on October 6th and claimed to be there until they were arrested on the 10th of Oct. They had run out of places to stay, having stayed at hotels furnished by different churches. He claimed they decided to call the Stapleton residence in Searcy on a whim, in hopes of acquiring Ray Stapleton's phone number in Wisconsin. Ray had informed Karash in August he was taking a teaching job in Wisconsin. Therefore, they assumed Ruby could provide Ray's new number. They were adamant about not knowing Ruby was missing. Ray had told investigators during his last conversation with Chandler in August, Chandler threatened if Ray didn't give him money, he "had another alternative." Was this alleged statement a precursor to Ruby's disappearance? Chandler and Karash deny threatening Ray and using any terms such as "we have another alternative." Karash states he hadn't had contact with Ray Stapleton since late August.

Thinking the relationship between the Doc and the two men might be a promising lead, the F.B.I. continued the interview with Ray. Ray told them a peculiar story, and the event had occurred prior to Ruby's kidnapping. The story ended with Ruby baking a pie for one of the accused kidnappers. Ray told investigators in late August, he and Mrs. Stapleton traveled to Little Rock for the purpose of servicing an automobile, and while there, met up with and had dinner with Gray Chandler. As police went through Karash and Chandlers things, they came across a letter written from Ray to Chandler from mid-August corroborating Ray's unusual story. It sounded like a friendly letter, inquiring about job prospects, but later in the investigation, police found out theirs wasn't just a platonic friendship.

The letter from police files obtained through FOIA states:
Dear Gray,
What have you been doing, Gray? What about the radio work possibility. I don't know why I'm asking you these questions. For I don't expect you to reply. It just seems natural to ask. Mrs. Stapleton and I expect to come to Little Rock Friday afternoon of this week. We shall want you to come eat with us somewhere, and I will call you early Friday morning about details. Do go with us and don't be nervous, just be your usual sweet self, and let us both enjoy you together. Take care of yourself now and we will be seeing you real, real soon.
Your friend, Doc.

In my research, I found Ray was referred to as "The Doc" and often referred to himself as "Doc" when conversing with his acquaintances. This letter implying Gray would be nervous to eat dinner with Ray and his wife caused me to stop and think. Why would he be nervous? There are many details regarding Ray, Chandler, and Karash's relationships that are explained more in depth in the later statements I have included near the end of this book.

Although Ruby and Ray did eat with Chandler at Frank's Cafeteria in Little Rock on Friday evening, Chandler claimed that was the last time he saw Mrs. Stapleton. As much as my curious mind wanted to know, no other details about what was discussed or what the atmosphere was like at dinner were found in the section of Ray's statement in the police files. When Ruby and Ray returned home after dinner with Chandler, Ruby told Ray she would bake Chandler a pie if Ray would "pick out the pecans." In his statement, Ray says he picked out the pecans, and she baked the pie for him to take to Chandler. This paints a scene in my mind. Ray sitting at the table carefully picking out pecans (shelling them?), and Ruby retrieving her apron, pulling out measuring cups, and starting the mixing of ingredients.

I wonder if things were strained in this moment. The knowledge of two letters marked with tension tells me things were not smooth on the home front. I wonder why Ruby would serve a pie to a man she hardly knows, especially if she suspected what Ray was up to with this man. I have also speculated if Ruby did not know, then perhaps she is trying to do her Christian duty in servitude by baking a pie for a person met with hard times. Or did she have a hunch this man Chandler was possibly connected in some way to the threats referred to in the letter Clarita read? It would be helpful to know the details about the men threatening Ray, but we will likely never know. Whatever her reasons, Ruby certainly had a giver's heart.

The next day, Ray went to Little Rock expecting to meet Chandler again and deposit the pie, but Chandler was nowhere to be seen. Chandler relayed later in his statement he was tired of waiting around for the Doc in the heat and went to meet other friends. The month of August was the last time the two men claimed to have had any contact with Ray Stapleton up until they contacted him on October 10th. Eventually, the police checked Karash and Chandler's alibi for the evening of October 8th. Hotel receipts, plus several eyewitnesses, placed them in Lubbock at the time of Ruby's kidnapping. A dead end for the investigators. It was all very confusing and provided little aid in solving Ruby's whereabouts.

The interview continued with Ray, investigators switching to the topic of finances. The police discovered Ruby had sold 4 properties to Harding College in the summer of 1963. Ruby's properties were located smack dab in the middle of Harding campus. Curiously, in the letter I mentioned before, the one Clarita had glanced over in Ruby's kitchen, a request was made by Ruby. She pleaded with Ray to not divorce her. She told him she would sell her properties to Harding and split the profit with him if he changed his mind about divorcing her. Cleary, he changed his mind for the time being and allowed her to sell the properties.

Ruby had previously gifted a house she owned next door to hers to her son Glen Dewey. Glen Dewey was approached by Dr. Benson to sell that house to Harding as well. Glen Dewey stated to police that Ruby arranged a meeting with Dr. Benson in her home and completed the sale. Glen Dewey was then given a small parcel of land from Ruby, coincidentally three miles from the Norge Launderama. He built his home on it, and that is where he was residing with his wife and 2 children at the time of Ruby's disappearance.

Harding used the purchased properties to pave way for a most significant structure. The aforementioned muddy puddles by Clarita would have been due to the construction on the new building next door to Ruby's house. The American Heritage building still stands today overlooking the big lawn, facing opposite of the administration building where the well-known lily pool resides. The grandiose structure houses a cafeteria, hotel, meeting rooms, and administrative offices.

In small towns, word travels fast, and many knew of the Stapleton's acquired wealth. In fact, there was an article in the Harding Bison, highlighting Harding's purchases from the Stapletons. Could this recent financial gain have any significance in her disappearance?

An excerpt from The Harding Bison Publication September 12th, 1963.

Construction has virtually begun on Harding College's New American Heritage Center and alumni Building. As soon as grading and leveling are finished, the actual construction will begin, probably in a week or two, stated President George E. Benson. The target date for completion is slated for August 1964, he added. The building will be the largest, most attractive, and offer the widest variety of services of all the structures on campus. It completes the quadrangle of buildings with the main campus as its center. Clearing the way for the $700,000 structure has involved the raising of four houses and the moving of three others. The four adjacent properties north of the campus were purchased from Doctor and Mrs. E.R. Stapleton for the building location. Two other properties were bought on Market Street to allow for entrance and parking space for the building.
[End of excerpt.]

Police continued asking Ray about his finances, questioning him about various wires and charges on his account. Ray claimed the wire transfers were to help friends who were down on their luck. Ray went on in the interview and gave accounts of monies "gifted" to "friends" over the course of a few years. When asked about a large sum of money recently wired out of Ray's account, he stated it was due to an illegal activity, and he refused to explain what it was used for or to who it was given. He said he would not incriminate himself or the other party. Ray admitted a short time later in the interview he had spent most of the money in question on an acquaintance who was rather special to him. That piqued my interest. It roused the investigators suspicions as well. I came across a letter addressed to the police department in Superior, Wisconsin from the ASP asking for all financial records regarding Ray Stapleton. The police were thoroughly investigating his finances in hopes of linking a clue to this mystery, but to their dismay, nothing concrete was found. The interview continued, and the subject changed from finances to personal lifestyle. He went on to give a colorful and descriptive second interview.

In his initial statement, he denied marital issues, but in fact there were ripples of trouble in the family dynamic. Deeper into his interview, he admitted to turbulence in the marriage. Although he did not admit the extent of his marital troubles. He was very quick to point out Ruby's flaws but seemed to leave out his own. A few years before Aunt Ruby was murdered my grandma witnessed Ray hitting Ruby across the face, on two separate occasions. My grandma was shocked and said she "made herself scarce and busied herself in the kitchen" and tried to avoid the situations all together. My grandma was living with Ruby while attending Harding college and was fearful of Ray after these events. My grandma remembered Ray as being volatile and angry during her stay there. She recalled Ray coming home from a church service and losing his cool when talking about George Benson, or others he held disdain for, and would shout expletives and shake his fists. Ray did not divulge those incidents to investigators.

The interview continued with Ray opening up about his personal life, rambling on a bit, giving excuses as to why things were troublesome. As mentioned before, Ray had been harboring a secret for quite some time. Once disclosed, this information unavoidably became a source of intrigue in the investigation. The secret Ray had kept hidden was the fact he was engaging in sexual acts with men and had been doing so for many years. Certain behavior in that era was considered taboo, and illegal in some states. Even though same sex attraction was a definite unacceptable thing back then, that was not the only thing raising detectives' eyebrows. Upon deeper investigation, it was learned there was a more sinister secret Ray was keeping.

Prior to Ruby's disappearance, my family members did not have knowledge of Ray's secret behavior. On one occasion, in my mother's childhood before Ruby died, her family visited Ray at his home in Texas, where he taught at a college. During their visit, they met a young man staying with my Uncle Ray in a spare bedroom. My mother's family was told the young man was a temporary boarder, renting a room from Ray, and nothing else. It appeared his secret was hiding in broad daylight. During the investigation, it was found out Ray had dozens of male roommates over the course of several years. It was his common practice to pick up younger men who were hitchhiking, much like he did with Chandler and Karash, and offer them a place to stay while they looked for work, etc. Ray told investigators a few of these men he was helping financially were essentially trying to blackmail the doc to keep him silent about the sexual things he was doing with them. Ray's interview continued to state key details in his personal life.

Excerpt- Continued notes from E.R. Stapleton Interviews

Investigators then questioned Doctor Stapleton about his associations with homosexuals, and he told a long and descriptive story about his past experience and admitted performing actual homosexual acts on numerous occasions with many individuals, most of whom he did not know the names, and some whose names were furnished. He lists several names, some who are students at colleges and some who are on faculty at Harding.

At this point in my research, I had to take a moment to process. The names listed dated all the way back to the 1930s up until the 1960s. Including the names of Karash and Chandler. I realize this might be of interest to the reader, but I am torn between listing the names or leaving them out. Although Ray had garnered himself quite a reputation at Harding, rumored to be nicknamed Sister Stapleton and Flossie for his feminine nature, not everyone was aware of his secret life. For reasons unknown, 9 years prior, Dr. Benson became aware of Ray's sexual liaisons. Professor Ray Stapleton didn't voluntarily relocate to take a job out of state; he was asked by Dr. George Benson to leave Harding because of his extracurriculars with male teachers and male students. Harding

University would not want that marking their untarnished name and would not have divulged that information publicly. Again, in the 1960s that kind of thing was disapproved of, especially at a Christian college.

Doc Stapleton's checkered relationships across the country created a mound of names investigators had to sift through to determine if any were valid suspects. The police were justified in wondering if his secret behavior had anything to do with Ruby's disappearance. Ray's statement went on to reveal more about a certain individual on the list he provided, who appeared to be a significant person to Ray. The man was the one Ray was spending most of his money on, as previously mentioned. This newly discovered information highlighted the confusion the investigators faced, forcing them to track down numerous potential suspects.

I read through the list of furnished names, deciding to use names that were publicly given at the time or might have relevance to the case.

Continued police notes marked as Supplement #7
Listed as facts

Roy Whitfield, now working as a missionary now and who at the time of these homosexual acts during the early 1930s, was a student at Harding College, Searcy, AR.

Clarence Heflinger, who at the time of these homosexual acts during 1951 was a professor at Harding College.

Douglas Martin, who lived in an apartment with Stapleton while Stapleton taught at Northeast Louisiana State College, Monroe, LA. And who attempted to blackmail Stapleton during the Commission of these homosexual acts.

Grady Bankhead, who lived with Stapleton while he taught at East Texas State College. Commerce, Texas.

Douglas Daugherty, who lived with Stapleton while he taught at East Texas State College, Commerce, Texas.

Billy Joe Rust, who lived with Stapleton while he taught at East Texas State College, Commerce, Texas.

Karl Karash, who is now in custody of the US Marshall at Lubbock, TX and he lived with Stapleton while he taught at Boone, NC.

Gray F Chandler, who is now in custody of the US Marshall at Lubbock, TX and who lived with Stapleton while he taught at Boone, NC.

Jack Irvine, who lived with Stapleton while he taught at Boone, North Carolina.

Dalon Dean Barnes lived with Stapleton when he taught at Boone, NC.

The name James Douglas Daugherty was not furnished voluntarily by Stapleton in this questioning and was obtained by investigators from a record of long-distance calls made by Stapleton during the past few months. Stapleton had completed his list of homosexuals whose names were known to him and whom he had enjoyed "affairs in my house" and had been in the process of trying to rack his brain to tell of any others that he might recall their names. Stapleton was given an opportunity to think for several minutes and then he made the statement that there were many others but that he could recall no other names and certainly had no long-prolonged affairs with any persons not already mentioned to us.

Stapleton was then asked if he knew Douglas Daugherty. He showed great surprise, raised up abruptly in his chair, and exclaimed, my word, man, where did you get that name? Investigators did not answer his question and then asked him what his relation with Douglas Daugherty had been.

Stapleton regained his composure and stated that he had met Douglas Daugherty after Daugherty had been pointed out to him by another homosexual who Stapleton refused to name and had approached Daugherty about performing homosexual acts with Stapleton. Daugherty consented and lived in Stapleton's house occasionally and rented rooms and at some time performed these acts in an automobile. Stapleton traveled with Douglas Daugherty to his home near Canton, TX and met his parents. On that occasion he learned that Douglas Daugherty was 15 years old. He told of visiting and seeing Daugherty intermittently for several years and giving him small sums of money. Buying his meals and paying for his bowling.

There are many details to his statement that are hard for me to digest. So basically, my Uncle Ray was, in what today's terms would crassly be called, a sugar daddy, with a dark secret? An underage boy was the object of his affection? The rhetorical questions are bouncing back and forth in my mind. Many questions to be quite honest. Was my Uncle Ray a predator? How many other underage boys did he have encounters with? Clearly from the information in Ray's statement, Ray did not want this information about James Douglas Daugherty to be known. When the police found out this information, they continued questioning him in great length.

Ray told them details about his relationship with Douglas Daugherty. Up until the day Ruby was abducted, Ray was in constant communication with the young man, Douglas Daugherty. He stated how much he loved this person and was willing to do anything to receive loving from him. Ray offered Daugherty a free ride to college if he would leave his common law wife and move in with Ray. Douglas Daugherty ended and restarted his relationship with his common law wife often, and Ray grew resentful. That pattern went on for a lengthy time, and at the time of Ruby's disappearance, Ray was fed up with Daugherty's indecisiveness. He felt Daugherty was choosing the woman over him. He presented the offer once more of a free college ride, but when he found out Daugherty moved back in with his common law wife, he rescinded his offer and said he was done with the whole situation. That was in October, the 9th to be exact.

On the morning after Ruby's disappearance, Ray sent a telegraph advising for Daugherty to contact him collect at his home in Searcy. Ray periodically visited the home he shared with Ruby, and vice versa, and it wouldn't appear strange for him to ask Daugherty to contact him there. Daugherty called collect, and Ray informed him Ruby was missing. Ray stated he was disappointed in how

Daugherty reacted, telling investigators his love interest did not give much of a concerned reaction. Ray questioned him about his common law wife, and that is when the conversation took place of Ray ending the relationship with Daugherty.

Ray shared something of even more interest to investigators. He claimed Daugherty and his common law wife were aware that Ray was a free spender and insinuated they might think he was worth more with Ruby out of the way. Ray relayed to the F.B.I. he was concerned for his wife's safety over the last year due to this. He claimed some of the other individuals he was associated with were aware of his wealth also, and if Ruby was out of the way, Ray would have easier access to Ruby's money to spend on them. He told investigators he never shared these fears of his with Ruby. It raises my suspicions as to if Ruby did in fact know these men could harm her because of the letters exchanged and because Ruby did seem nervous in the time before her disappearance. The claim by Ray created a solid motive, but ultimately there was still nothing tying Ray or his acquaintances to Ruby's disappearance.

Ray then told officers a long and detailed story of why he was practicing *"homosexual acts"* and blamed the matter solely on his wife. He said Ruby was the reason he was with men. He claimed living with Ruby became unbearable, as her housekeeping was atrocious. He stated that she stopped caring about her personal hygiene, and the house was always in disarray. When questioned as to why he was no longer working at Harding, he claimed he only left due to differences in opinion of policies. The question remains still, whether Ruby was attuned to Ray's furtive lifestyle. It is easy to speculate, but as always, the devil is in the details. And the devilish thing is, there are details pointing to her being fully aware and other details showing glaring proof she did *not* know of her husband's secret rendezvous.

In talking with a retired detective about Ruby's case and the lingering question of how much she knew about Ray's actions, he stated in all his years of detective work, wives always seem to suspect and most often know about this kind of thing. We can know for sure Ruby's extended family had not even an inkling of Ray's secrets at the time of Ruby's death. Family might have assumed there could be trouble in the marriage, hence the move out of state by Ray years prior, but never would have imagined the reason why.

In those days, people tried hard to keep from airing their dirty laundry. Especially dirty laundry of that nature. People operated on a don't ask don't tell mentality.

If Ruby did know of his secrets, she was skilled at keeping their personal life out of people's minds and mouths. She would not have wanted anything jeopardizing her position at the college or affecting her children in any way. By staying with Ray, Ruby preserved her employment and her fellowship within the Churches of Christ, because Ray's secret was just as taboo as a divorce would be in the eyes of her peers. I don't think we will ever know for sure how much Ruby knew of Ray's secrets.

The F.B.I. tracked down Ray's much younger love interest, James Douglas Daugherty, and Daugherty claimed he was at work in California at the time of Ruby's disappearance. The F.B.I. confirmed his alibi for the night of October 8th and found nothing tying him or his common law wife to Ruby's disappearance. Daugherty's brother had taken his car across country on a road trip the week Ruby went missing, and investigators were thorough in retracing their steps. It appeared as if the brother could have stopped at Searcy on the night of October 8th as it was in the direct route he was traveling. The amount of time it took them to reach their destination of Pennsylvania did not add up with the time frame needed to abduct and kill Ruby, though. There were lengthy interviews with Daugherty's family members. Specifically, his mother and brother, and yet again, the detectives hit a brick wall.

Included in the back of this book are statements from the Daugherty family, and further information regarding the investigation into the family members is there as well.

Continuing the interview, Ray gave explicit detail on the types of things he did with each person he was involved with, referring to them as "petting parties." One individual, Douglas Dwaine Martin, had met Ray hitchhiking in the spring of 1962 and had been residing with him for a time, while Ray was teaching at the Appalachian State College in Boone, North Carolina. Ray claimed Martin was tiring of the petting parties and tried to blackmail him. Ray claimed he tried to call his bluff, which resulted in Martin turning him in to the police.

Martin claimed Ray was taking advantage of him, sexually, and other students at the college there in Boone. Martin reported Ray for his behavior with the young boys at college, and police paid a visit to Ray at his home. They found multiple pictures scattered all over his house depicting male genitalia, and Ray was arrested. Ray told investigators he was able to escape persecution by agreeing to the police in Boone that he would "leave the area and never come back." Ray painted himself as the victim in the situation, saying Martin tried to ruin other men's lives by false claims. But he admitted giving Martin money for performing sexual acts with him. Another hopeful lead turned into frustration as investigators tracked down and even gave Douglas Dwaine Martin a polygraph. He was cleared by his alibi of being out of town at work and passed his polygraph according to police files. All those salacious stories coming to light were not bringing investigator's any closer to discovering what happened to Ruby.

◆◈◆

As investigators sifted through the layers of Doc Stapleton's statement, the family members were faced with this bombshell being brought to light. The revelation told by Dr. Benson that frantic day to Clarita and her parents exploded into the laps of family and has continued to be a lingering point of curiosity and reason for suspicion all these years. The information regarding Ray and his suitors was so scandalous for its time, investigators were valid for wondering if there was more to Ray they would uncover. In the early 1960s same sex relations were still illegal and, in many places, punishable by jail time. Investigators wonder about other illegal activities Ray was involved with.

If we look at Ray through the eyes of the law today, he would not be guilty of a crime for having same sex attraction. What stands out though, is his behavior with underage boys was and still is a crime, paying for sex was and still is a crime, and the way he described in his statements picking up young vulnerable boys is the classic definition of grooming. This is what makes Ray appear as someone who was willing to go to great lengths to commit these acts. The investigators wonder just how far was he willing to go? Could he have been a part of a secret trafficking ring?

One observation made by my granddad in the early 1960s gives cause to speculate. My granddad had purchased a new Cadillac and was visiting Ruby at her home in Searcy. While he was visiting, Ray also came to Searcy for a visit. Ray had recently purchased a new Cadillac as well. In doing what men often do, they were comparing their cars, miles, design, etc. My granddad noticed Ray's mileage was exceedingly high compared to his own, and they had purchased the cars at the same time. My granddad pondered if the miles were high because Ray did live out of state and traveled some back and forth to Searcy. Taking that into consideration, the mileage, in his opinion, still exceeded far above what would have been normal. Even he as a traveling salesman, my granddad hadn't put near as many miles on his car.

In the police files, I discovered statements that confirmed Ray was putting many miles on his car, being out and about frequently. Some statements from men living with Ray detailed how Ray would go out many times a week at night, patrolling the highways looking for vulnerable hitchhikers to perform sex acts with him. My granddad's suspicion that Ray was also transporting people across the country with the purpose of performing sex acts with others in the same "club" was never proven, but it's another interesting point in this case to be scrutinized. Ray himself admitted to traveling to Texas with the intention of performing sex acts, and on one of those trips, he was introduced to Daugherty. Ray was silent as to who pointed Daugherty out to him, and one can gather there were many others practicing criminal behavior Ray did not want to incriminate. The extended family may not have known about Ray's taboo lifestyle, but my granddad was privately suspicious about what Ray was up to but never would have dared shared something like that to the women in the family.

It is important to note, even though Ray, today, would have more than likely been arrested for the criminal acts he admitted to, there was no concrete evidence tying him to Ruby's murder, and he was never held responsible for Ruby's death. We do know he had a rock-solid alibi, and nothing has been proven that he took part in orchestrating her murder. We would not be doing Ruby any justice if we latched onto this idea that since Ray was practicing criminal behavior, he must have committed the crime. There are many theories and plenty of others who could have motive.

We all have things that shaped our childhood; some memories

we'd rather push to the corners of our mind. For me, this was the rumor about Uncle Ray, the infamous character who I knew not. I recall a feeling of disdain for Uncle Ray from the things I heard growing up. Never having met him, I could only drum up in my mind what a child was capable of. I'd seen villains on TV, the bad guys in creepy spacesuits who tried to hurt E.T. or the evil Doctor Jekyll from the old film. Ray was the villain in my mind, holding the key to Ruby's death and never held accountable. I was told he was "vile, evil" and a host of other things.

From the moment my family's suspicions were confirmed about Ray's deviant behavior, every unscrupulous person my family encountered became "just like Uncle Ray." Be it their behavior, their accent, their mannerisms, if they were thought to have done anything morally wrong, they became him. I always heard the phrase, "Oh he's just like Uncle Ray." Growing up I was confused as to why there was no justice if it was common knowledge who committed this crime. I realize now this was not an open and shut case.

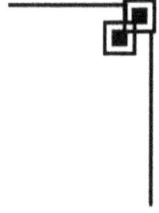

~ CHAPTER FIVE ~

Thrown Out with The Wash

Body at Bull Creek

As the detectives continued the hard work of tracking down every tip to locate the missing professor, there were murmurings and speculation in abundance. There wouldn't be an update for 11 agonizing days.

On October 19th, the search for Ruby shifted to a search for her killer. At 5:15 p.m. on that cool autumn night, twenty-one-year-old outdoorsman Jerry V. Bass came across Ruby Stapleton's nude, decomposed body. Dumped in a dry creek bed, Ruby had been inhumanely left on a mound of debris. Discarded and thrown over the edge like trash or soiled clothes. It was a gruesome display of sheer callousness.

The body was located down Apple Road, just off the old McCrae-Beebe Road, a few feet from the embankment to Bull Creek. Bull Creek, also known as Bull Bayou, was a waterway that ran between

Searcy and its sister town of Beebe, the area being fifteen miles from the washeteria. Bass stated he was sure it was a body and hastily went to get his father. His father thought maybe his son had seen a rotting animal, but when his father saw the remains, he knew instantly it was the missing Harding professor. The shock of black hair seen in the dirt couldn't belong to anyone else. A call was made, and a state trooper came out. The intrigue and mystery of this crime deepened even further.

Jerry V. Bass

In my diligence for seeking accurate information, I reached out to many people along the way. One of these people of importance for me to contact was Jerry V. Bass. Feeling as if I were searching for a needle in a haystack, I delved into my search. Much to my excitement, I was able to find the man who had come upon my aunt's remains. I contacted him in September of 2023, and he graciously agreed to meet with me. I was so thankful for this unique opportunity that when he gave me directions to his home, the very same day I made contact, I was enroute within the hour. I was eager to meet this man whom I felt like I had heard about my whole life.

Down a narrow gravel lane, set back from the road, his country home was shrouded in trees. Pulling up I could see a small man standing in the yard patiently awaiting my arrival. With his John Deer cap, plaid button-down shirt, and faded blue jeans, Jerry Bass was every bit of what I imagined him to be. A good ole country boy of eighty-one years. A bit of white hair peeking out beneath his cap, I felt an instant liking for him. This man was a living connection to the past. Mr. Bass merged our grief into some type of closure we would not have found, had he not walked that secluded path some sixty years ago. His discovery, that warm October day, did not help us know the why as to what happened to Aunt Ruby, but it did provide the what, when, and where; and for that we will forever be grateful.

After making introductions, my daughter handed him a small gift bag. Twenty years old at the time, my daughter, Aryanna, had accompanied me on this spur of the moment road trip and was eager to gift him the muffins we had bought along the way. He looked perplexed and held the quickly stuffed gift bag in midair, as if not sure what to do with it. Aryanna smiled and told him, "We just wanted to give you something to show our gratitude for meeting with us." I made sure to inform him it was just a couple of muffins, and he seemed disarmed at that. He tucked our small sacrifice of gratitude in his truck, and we followed him to the 'place of discovery,' a short drive down the road, across a small intersection. He kindly and assuredly walked me through his memory of the day many years ago.

A very important thing worth noting in this mystery is the discreet location of discovery. It was very secluded. When I initially reached Mr. Bass by phone, one of the first things he stated to me was that he had always wondered how someone could have known to place her body there at the creek. It was not a place you would drive by and see from the road. Someone would have had prior knowledge of the narrow, hidden path to know it existed. He wonders if the perpetrator, prior to the abduction, purposely scouted out an area deep in the woods to find a secluded place to conceal their crime. And if so, how did they come to know about this spot?

In the description found in the police report, I noticed the term "dim road" relating to the place of discovery. My interest was aroused as I was not familiar with that term. I looked it up and found several definitions: An unpaved road that has had little to no use for a length of time and is mostly overgrown; a road that is not used frequently and may have overgrowth *making it hard to see*; a road that is unpaved and *not easily visible*, and the list goes on.

My mind shouts, *"Not easily visible."* This definition solidified in my mind that someone would have been familiar with the area to know about this dim road. It also appeared to be quite a drop off, so anyone driving up to it wouldn't venture down, assuming it was a steep drop off and not thinking it was accessible. The killer most definitely would have had prior knowledge of the road…and knew it could be the perfect place to hide a body. Affirming my thoughts about this hidden side road, Mr. Bass continues in his memory detailing that day.

"No one would have walked down to the creek to dispose of the body," he stated. "They would have thrown her off the edge and there had to have been two men, if not a third, to hoist her that far into the creek." He tells me he had been squirrel hunting down one length of Bull Bayou the week before, and then on October 19th, where the creek runs under a bridge, he crossed over and continued down the same side. Walking down the secluded path about 100 yards in, he saw her body laying across the shallow creek. Looking out over the creek today you can easily see the drop off as it was all those years ago. Steep cliffs line the edge of the creek, the embankment dropping straight down to about 13 feet.

When he caught a glimpse of her sprawled body, he stood for a moment trying to understand what he was seeing, realization setting in that this was most likely the missing woman he had heard about in the news. When we talked by phone, I asked him to confirm it was him who found my aunt's remains, and I heard a woman's voice in the background (presumably his wife's) state matter-of-factly, *"He smelled her first before seeing her."* The extreme humidity and length of time her body was left out in the elements caused rapid and advanced decomposition.

Mr. Bass answered me quickly and just as matter-of-factly as the voice in the background. "Yes, I found her and have wondered all these years how they knew to put her body there."

I can't explain it, but I felt as if he had been waiting for this phone call. There was a hint of excitement and bewilderment in his voice. When I asked him when he would be available to meet with me, I did not expect him to say that day. It was as if he wanted the meeting just as badly as I did.

We stood at the bridge's edge, and he continued telling me about his memory of what he did after discovering the body. He stated in, what I would affectionately describe as, his Arkansas drawl,

"I was by myself, and I parked my truck, about where I have mine now, and I backed up to turn around…and the road is pretty steep there…and I left some pretty good rifts when I come out of there. I went and told my dad, and he called the state trooper and they come out and we walked down there and found her."

As Mr. Bass motioned to an area further down the creek, I strained my eyes trying to see the spot through the hanging branches. I   asked, "She'd been out there awhile, and she was pretty decomposed, right?"

And he replied, "Ya about 11 days I guess it was."

I asked, "Did you know it was the missing professor pretty much right away?"

He answered matter-of-factly, "Sure did... sure did..." His voice trailing off.

I asked him "Could you see her hair?"

He said in his quiet Arkansas drawl, "Yap, you could see everything, she was layin' face up, didn't have any... had no clothes on." He started to speak again but paused, looking silently out over the creek, and then continued saying, "Somebody did a gruesome thing there... bad deal there that they never got caught... they'll get caught somewhere. A lotta that stuff going on people were gettin away with it. Sheriff's office rumored to be corrupt back then. Maybe she knew too much."

My mind was racing with all the things I had heard up until that point, and the general consensus was Ruby had been silenced. His statement was not surprising to me as I had heard the claim about the White County Sheriff's office before, from some of the citizens I interviewed who live in Searcy. It is hard to know if it's idle speculation or if it's a widely known secret for the quaint little town of Searcy. Other murders seem to have a level of suspicion surrounding them as well and rumors of crooked dealings with the sheriff's office back then were a dime a dozen. The question we do not know the answer to, is what could Ruby have known too much of?

I inquired, "Did you ever go visit that spot again?"

He replied, "Oh maybe a time or two, maybe to show someone." Then he pointed to the creek again out over the bridge and said, "It looks just like that dry spot right there aways. There was probably a little bit of water, and they may have thought there was more water and if there was, she never would have been found."

My investigative journalist daughter in training commented on how the dark night would have also been hiding the fact there wasn't water covering the length of the creek, and Mr. Bass agreed. The killers possibly thought they were disposing of the body in a few feet of water, not knowing it wasn't very deep and not expecting the drought that ensued. The week Ruby went missing, there happened to be a drought, and in those 11 days the water dried up, exposing her otherwise undetected body.

The overgrowth on the formerly secluded, dim road made it inaccessible to walk through. My daughter walked across the short bridge and ventured her way down the opposite side of the creek on a clearer path, hoping to see the area where Ruby was left. We followed her lead, being careful of the prickly briar, but as we were traipsing along Mr. Bass got poked by one of those unforgiving thorns. I glanced down to see a bright red drop forming at the tip of Mr. Bass's finger. I let him know we had tissue in the car if needed, and he laughed at that.

We stood at the banks edge looking down over the sparsely covered creek, more dry spots than wet, each of us in our own thoughts. Mr. Bass gestured to the spot, as best he could remember, where her body lay sixty years ago. Aways across the creek, closer to the side opposite from where we were standing, was where he found her. I captured a picture of Mr. Bass looking out over the creek, seeing the memory in his eyes of all those years ago and thinking about what he must have felt in that moment.

As we walked back to the safety of the open road, meaning no more spider webs and threats of ticks, we watched our step as there were bits of debris everywhere. The area looks very similar to how it looked sixty years ago, thick with vegetation, steep drop offs, standing water in a mostly dry creek, and scattered debris. We walked the few steps back to our cars parked off the side of the bridge and stood around as if not wanting to say goodbye but not knowing why we would stay. We admired the sun shining brightly through the heavy vegetation.

I commented, "Without you finding her, Ruby's family never would have had a burial. In that sense, you gave us closure…Even though it must have been traumatic for you to come upon her remains, we are grateful that you did."

He humbly replied, "Well. Thank you very much. It was sure nice to know you."

I would like to think in some small way, my daughter and I were a comfort to him after all those years he was forced to live with the gruesome memory.

Mr. Bass is a vital piece to this puzzle and gave me helpful observations. He stated emphatically the perpetrator would have been familiar with the area and one or more accomplices would have been needed to place Ruby in the creek. I echo his sentiment in that, whoever did this will pay for this crime one way or another. I curiously asked him if he believed in God, and he said he sure does.

Once back in the car, I remarked to my daughter how strange that now the man who found Ruby, and Ruby herself, had shed blood in the same place. I don't know why my mind makes these eerie observations. My daughter looked at me with wide eyes and said, "It's a sign, but I sure don't know what for."

Turns out Mr. Bass and I both had minor inconveniences that day. When I arrived home that night, I was dismayed to find a tick latched onto my leg. This city girl has an extreme fear of ticks, and I mean, a heart gripping, heart stopping, fear of ticks. I rolled my eyes and said to myself, chuckling, *anything for you Ruby.*

As I pulled the tick off my leg, I reflected on my time with Jerry V. Bass. His final words had left their mark on me. Before we got into our cars to leave the place of discovery, we turned once more to look out over the creek down to where her body was discovered. A shadow drifted across Jerry's eyes. He declared softly, "She went through hell... she went through thunder."

Jerry Bass standing near the place where he found Ruby's body
September 2023

Squirrel hunter finds body near Beebe Saturday

Weary law enforcement officials, climaxing ten days of fruitless investigation into what could never be proved to be more than a possible kidnaping, today had the positive identification of a nude and decomposed body found in a dry creek bed near Beebe as that of missing Harding English teacher, Mrs. E. R. Stapleton.

"We've had to work almost in the dark from the start on this case," Sheriff Jack Price said this morning, "because until the body was found we didn't really have a crime to investigate."

Chief Deputy Sheriff Benson Robbins, who has been in charge of the investigation, said that the body was found by a squirrel hunter, Jerry Bass, 21, of Beebe, shortly after 5 p.m. Saturday. It was found in the dry bed of Bull Creek on the Old Searcy Highway about two miles northeast of Beebe, only a few hundred yards off a heavily-traveled U.S. Highway 67. The body was in a wooded area but was only a few feet from a dirt road that turns off the gravel road and parallels Bull Creek, Robbins said.

The body was rushed to the University of Arkansas Medical Center in Little Rock, where an autopsy was performed. County Coroner Allan Foster said that the autopsy report showed a wad of cotton "about the size of a man's fist" lodged in the throat. The throat also showed a fracture which indicated strangulation as the cause of

MRS. E. R. STAPLETON

criminal assault was not established due to the elapsed time and the advanced state of composition, authorities said.

Members of the Stapleton family this morning completed plans for funeral services to be held in the Harding College auditorium at 10 a.m. Wednesday. Mrs. Stapleton, a member of the Harding faculty since 1952, was last seen at a washateria on South Main Street at 10:15 p.m. on October 6. She had come to the washateria from the home of her son, Glen Dewey Stapleton, on Highway 67 South after stopping by her home on East Center Avenue to pick up some additional clothes. She was reported missing by her family at midnight.

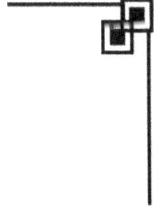

~ CHAPTER SIX ~

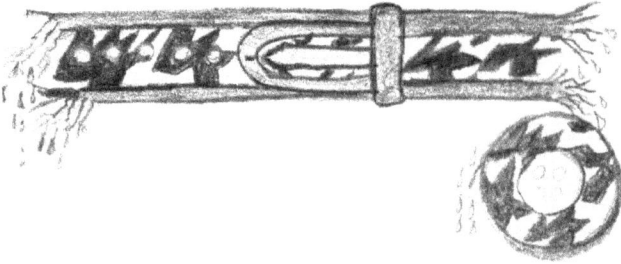

Heavy Load

B ack in Nebraska on October 19th,1963 my mother's family eagerly waited for any updates on Ruby's vanishing. My grandma had just walked in after purchasing eggs from a friend when she received the news Ruby's body had been discovered. Still cradling the eggs in her arms, she gathered her children while weeping and told them the fate of their precious great aunt Ruby. My mother recalled at that moment, she thought to herself, "She is like a mother hen gathering her chicks under the shelter of her protective wing." What a poignant thought for an eight-year-old.

It was the moment life changed in my mother's family. Fear was instilled in an already uncertain world of evil, and from that moment on, life was never the same. For many years my grandma was afraid to let my mother and her siblings play outside without supervision. My mother remembers a time when there was a dark car driving slowly by my mother's home, and my grandma had let her youngest out to ride his bike. She became hysterical and fetched him immediately. This crime has had lasting effects on so many people.

My granddad, grandma, my mother, and her siblings traveled the twelve hours with urgency to Searcy after hearing the news. It was a long, solemn drive. When they arrived, my granddad asked to see Ruby's remains (I would imagine he demanded, not asked). He wanted to be sure it was his beloved Ruby, possibly holding out hope it was a mistake. It's unimaginable what the family must have been going through. This was, and is, the most tragic thing ever to hit our family.

Once my granddad confirmed it was Aunt Ruby, my grandma tearfully said, "How can you be sure, knowing how long Ruby was exposed to the elements?" He replied, "I knew it was her by the Lowery legs."

Lowery lips and Lowery legs. Two expressions I often heard growing up. My grandma made the observation that my daughter Daisie inherited the perfectly shaped cupids bow and plump bottom lip from the Lowery side of the family. I'll never forget my grandma proclaiming with delight upon meeting her new great granddaughter, "She has the Lowery lips!" Daisie is my only daughter with dark hair and brown eyes, and we have always remarked on her strong resemblance to Aunt Ruby.

The genetic characteristic of having shapely and strong legs was also a family trait that seemed to be easily identifiable. I am sure my grandma never imagined it would be a way to identify her loved one who had been murdered. One more detail of this terrible event making it all the more real.

Meanwhile, earlier, down in Searcy on October 19th, another somber scene was unfolding. Some of the family was gathered at Ruby's residence with Mary Claire, still awaiting word on her missing mother. The doorbell rang, and it was a woman with her young daughter. The mother and daughter had brought food to the Stapleton home. The common practice of a community bringing food to sick or grieving family was going on full force. Compassionate friends of the family had sprung into action following Ruby's disappearance. At this point many people had the same idea and the food was bountiful.

As the family looked around for a place to set the food, the doorbell rang again. This time it was a member of law enforcement. He needed to speak to the family right away. The small group stood together as a scrap of belt and a small button were held up for the children of Ruby Stapleton to examine. The fabric on the belt was the easily recognizable black and white houndstooth pattern. Twenty-year-old Mary Claire confirmed the piece of severed belt matched the dress her mother was wearing the night she went missing. She now knew her mother had been found dead.

Shocked cries rang out. The young bystander delivering food stood pensively next to her mother, watching this interaction. She was tormented by this scene. Preferring to keep her identity to herself, the now older woman confided in me, *"To this day, I have never worn that pattern of fabric since I was there at the Stapleton home that night."* She shared with me that she also had trouble sleeping by herself for many years, even up until she got married. Ruby's murder has left a trail of sadness and torment for many involved.

❖❖

During the search for Ruby, Mary Claire and Clarita had provided a description of Ruby's clothing and accessories she had on the last night of her life. I've inserted the description below as found in police files.

Supplement #15

A description of the clothing worn and the articles in possession of the victim on the night of her disappearance are enclosed as Supplement #15 with this report.

The victim's two children and her niece, Clarita Bartley, describe the victims dress as follows.

Made of thin cotton material, white background and irregular shaped black figures which form an irregular checked design. This dress was fitted with a straight skirt and belt of matching material.

She was wearing shoes described as black flats pointed toe and worn in appearance described as about size 6.

Her underclothing consisted of full slip, bra, panty girdle and brief type panty.

She wore no jewelry except possible plain black earrings and was carrying a black plastic purse finished to look like very soft grain leather, the purse was about 12 inches long, 5 inches in height is a clutch type with silver finish snap at the top center and silver finish band extending across the top of the purse and down each side to the hinge.

It's not hard to imagine what Ruby's purse and dress could have looked like. To me it seemed quite fashionable. I would love to recreate this look, and I recently purchased myself some houndstooth earrings that serve as another way to keep my beautiful Aunt Ruby's memory alive. I've heard it said when something is brought to your attention, you see more of it. In the matter of the houndstooth dress, I have never seen that pattern more in my life. Since I discovered houndstooth was the last print Ruby wore, I've seen it on clothes, chairs, curtains, purses, even wallpaper. For a while everywhere I looked, I saw a houndstooth pattern. Every time I would see the print, my mind would fill with information from the police files, and I would feel an eagerness to rush back home to work some more. Another ironic sign, propelling me on this venture.

◆◆

Clarita Bartley had gone to a movie showing at the Harding campus and was not at the Stapleton residence when the police delivered the fate of Aunt Ruby. She shared with me her memory of finding out Ruby had been found.

Clarita upon hearing of Aunt Ruby's fate as told to me.
Harding had movie nights every Friday night and no matter what Hollywood movie it was, they would have to stop and change the reel. They only had one reel one projector and it would stop in the middle and they would change the reel. That was typical. Jerry had said let's go to the movies, you need to get out. I went to the movie and when the film stopped, I didn't think it was unusual but all of a sudden, the house lights went on and Dr. Benson was walking along the stage. I knew immediately she had been found and then he announced that the body of Ruby Stapleton had been found. (Clarita's voice cracked as she shared this with me, and my eyes filled with tears.) *She continued, "I immediately jumped up and went*

to his office and he apologized over and over again for announcing it in that way. He said, "Clarita, I thought you might be in the audience, but I didn't want to call your name out" and I said, "Well that's ok" and he told me what he knew."

Delivering the news to a crowded room full of loyal, hopeful, anxious students had to be difficult. I can imagine the gasps from the crowd as they heard the dreadful news. I am reminded of a time when I was younger. I lived in the small town of Harrison, AR for about two years until I was catapulted across the country to the Land of Enchantment, a.k.a. New Mexico. I was attending a weekly church service in Harrison when a church member interrupted the speaker to announce the sudden passing of a special young man from our small church/community. Brandon Burlsworth, a well-known aspiring college athlete, was killed instantly when his car collided with a semi-truck on a curvy road to his hometown of Harrison AR. He was young and taken too soon. I will never forget the announcer at church pausing while someone walked up to the podium and delivered the news. I imagine the gasps and cries of shock I heard that night were very similar to the reaction in the Harding auditorium. Nothing prepares you for that type of tragedy.

Dr. Benson encouraged Clarita and Mary Claire to keep on with their studies, saying Aunt Ruby surely wouldn't have wanted them to drop out. Clarita moved into the dorms while Ray stayed with his daughter Mary Claire in the house. Clarita stated for months after the murder, she would walk the short jaunt over to the police station and check with investigators to see if they had any new developments in the case. In talking to residents of Searcy that lived there in 1963, I learned Halloween was essentially cancelled, and most people were afraid to leave their house after dark. Women were especially afraid and took great measures for safety. The town was frozen in fear. Would the killer strike again? Was someone else next on this killers list? Imaginations and worse case scenarios were looming in people's minds. It was a scary time for the little community of Searcy.

❖

Family and friends came from many places to pay their respects. My mother and her family arrived in Searcy and attended church with some of the local family, as was their custom. The familiar sounds and sights in the church building brought little comfort. No one had answers, but everyone had questions. As my grandparents dropped Mary Claire back off at her home, they saw the curtain from the window move ever so slightly to reveal a glimpse of a figure peering through the front window. Ray was waiting for his daughter to come home. Mary Claire got out of the car and went inside to her father. My grandparents lingered before they slowly drove away while wondering what other secrets, if any, were in that house?

◆◆◆

Classes were cancelled once again for the beloved Professor, only this time it was to lay her soul to rest. On October 23rd, family and friends gathered to full capacity in the college auditorium to say their final goodbye to their favorite professor, friend, and relative. Harding Chorus sang songs chosen by the family. Clarita remembers Ray Stapleton as he was at the funeral. He sang with gusto during the songs and later, in the privacy of family, exclaimed with an edge of excitement, "Well at least she wasn't sexually abused!" It was a curious thing to say because the coroner had not been able to determine that matter one way or another at that point.

Dr. Benson read Ruby's obituary and stated in part, "Her friendly smile and genuine interest in students influenced for good thousands of young lives."

The Dean of students, L.C. Sears, addressed the crowd saying, "I feel that Mrs. Stapleton was one of the most loyal and dedicated teachers that was ever on the Harding campus and was one of the best loved. No one kept up with the students after they left Harding as well as she."

Ruby was one of those special kinds of teachers known for having an excellent rapport with her colleagues and students in part because of her friendly smile and helpful attitude. She was devout in her Christian upbringing and held her faith in high regard in every aspect of her life. You could say everyone loved Miss Ruby and she would be the last person you would think to be killed in such a heinous way. After the fanfare of a grand funeral and final goodbyes, police were no closer to solving the mystery of Ruby's death.

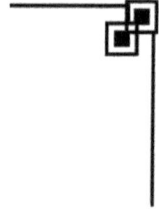

~ CHAPTER SEVEN ~

Hung Out to Dry

The Autopsy

As the college is processing the fact their much-loved professor is not coming back, the police on the other side of town are deep in the investigation. Using Ruby's dental records, she was positively identified. Allen Foster, coroner for White County, performed the autopsy on Oct 19th, citing the cause of death as suffocation or strangulation. A wad of high-grade cotton was found stuck tight in her throat. It was said to be the type you would get at a fabric store or a type of cotton cleaning rag that could also be found at places such as gas stations. One can assume it was used as a gag to keep her silent, but the fist sized wad of cotton was shoved so far down her throat, it was still intact on the day of discovery, causing the coroner to question if the cotton ultimately ended her life.

According to the autopsy, her hyoid bone was broken and could be the result of either manual strangulation or the cotton stuck tight in her throat. I briefly discussed this case with a retired homicide detective from my area. When I told him she had a gag shoved down her throat, he quickly stated that often when someone uses a gag it is used for more than just silencing any screams, it has a more symbolic reason. He stated that someone obviously wanted to "shut her up." I had barely told him any details about the case, and it was intriguing to me his initial thought was the same as many others.

Left outside to rot in the October elements, the body had been exposed for 11 days. The autopsy report, included later in this book, details the advanced state of decomposition the body was in at the time of discovery. The damage the elements caused had taken away any chance of determining if Ruby had been sexually assaulted. But the coroner was able to determine Ruby's body had cuts running up the length of her torso from her lower abdomen and fanned out across her upper chest. The cuts were made by an unknown sharp instrument. Also noted in Rudy's file was that her bra and belt had been severed with an unknown sharp instrument.

Another mystery that remains is if the cuts were a result of sexual mutilation or if the cuts were from removing her clothing. The textbook definition of criminal mutilation regarding a person states: the intentional infliction of physical abuse designed to cause serious permanent disfigurement or permanent or protracted loss or impairment of the functions of any bodily member or organ, where the offender relishes the infliction of the abuse, evidencing debasement or perversion. While this crime is heinous in nature, the cuts do not automatically mean they were sexually motivated. The cuts were reported to be shallow, not deep lacerations. I reached out to a cold case investigator from the Arkansas State Police and asked if she could somehow find out if the cuts were made postmortem, but I had no luck in my inquiry.

Next to the body they found a severed piece of her bra, where the cups meet in the middle part. The cuts made across her chest could have been from slicing off the bra. When I first read the report about the cuts on the body, I thought about her attire. I imagined she would have been wearing a girdle (body smoothing undergarment) or spanx, as we call it today. I was correct in my thinking, coming across that very information later in the reports.

If you know anything about spanx, they are impossible to take off easily. I imagine it would have been a challenge to remove Ruby's undergarment quickly, so the perpetrator may have decided to hastily cut through the fabric. Taking clothes would cause the body to be less likely to be identified if ever found. In 1963 DNA was not a threat to a criminal yet, so the removal of clothing and personal items was a common way criminals tried to cover their tracks.

The police record a vivid description of finding her body and the condition of her remains in their files copied below.

Police Files listed as Facts.
At 5:15 p.m. October 19th, 1963, a witness found the victim's body lying in the soft dirt of a dry creek bed at the bottom of a soft dirt bank that measures 13 feet in height. The top of this bank is on a level plain and 22 feet west of a dim dirt road that parallels and follows Bull Bayou. This creek bed is covered with vegetation and fallen leaves. A piece of driftwood of an undetermined length and a diameter of 1 1/4 inches at a point where it intersects a direct line from the body to the top of the bank, is located on this Creek bank and situated in an area about half the distance from the brink to the body and parallels the Creek bed. This piece of driftwood is broken in the area where it intersects the direct line from the bank to the body, and the broken piece remains attached to the rest of the driftwood and points in the direction of the body. A measured distance of 389 feet extends north between the area of the dim road, immediately adjacent to the spot where the body was found and the old McRae Beebe Rd.
The victim's body was found lying on her back, her head toward the creek bank and her feet toward the creek bed. The left leg was outstretched, the right leg was bent at the knee, outward, until the bottom of the right foot was parallel with the left knee. The head was turned to the left until the left side of the face rested on the ground. The left arm was extended until the upper arm was in line with the shoulder and the forearm was bent at the elbow at an angle near 90 degrees. The back of the entire left arm and left hand rested on the ground, and the fingers of this hand are loosely clinched. The right arm was bent at the elbow in an angle, permitting the right hand to

be concealed under the right side of the back at the waist. A shallow cut extends from the area of the vagina up the front center of the torso to a point 5 inches below the throat. Another shallow cut angles up the chest and across the upper area of the left breast to the left collarbone. Three additional shallow cuts angle from the center of the torso at the midriff, extending up across the left chest and upper area of the left breast. A search of the immediate area revealed a button located on the creek bank in the area immediately above the body and below the brink of this bank. A section of belt, containing the buckle, and measuring about 6 inches in length, was located in the creek bed at the bottom of the bank and immediately adjacent to the body. Microscopic examination of this section of belt reveals that the belt was severed by a sharp instrument. One half of a brassiere severed in the area between the cups was located under the victim's body. The belt and button have been identified by the victim's daughter as being attached to the dress worn by the victim on the night of her disappearance.
End of excerpt

Criminal profilers provide much information on understanding crime scenes. It is known that many times the way a body is discarded shows insight into the mind of the killer. If the killer has a direct tie to the victim, they will often cover up the victim with a blanket or something similar. This behavior is associated with a feeling of regret and has been given the term "undoing." Studies show when a perpetrator exercises remorse, they have some sort of connection to the victim, and it is not random. In the case of Ruby, her body being left out in the elements doesn't seem to fit with the theory of a remorseful killer. The way she was callously dumped would appear the killer or killers were acting in haste, trying to rid themselves of the body quickly, not acting out of emotions or regret.

It is hard to understand the mind of a killer, as all crimes differ from one to the next. It is important to look at all the evidence in determining the motivation behind a crime. The removal of clothes points to a crime sexual in nature but also points to a criminal covering their tracks. Many things to take into consideration when investigating a crime. I wonder if Ruby's team of investigators created a criminal profile using some of these clues or what methods they used in determining if this was sexually motivated or not.

One article I discovered gives insight and details on the main two types of killers, classified as organized and unorganized. I find articles like these fascinating and would hope they might shed light on elements of this case. Below is an excerpt from an article written by **Scott Bonn, Ph.D.** and gives an in depth look at profilers using crime scenes as a window to the killer's mind. Which in turn, could potentially lead investigators to a criminal profile to use in cases. You can read the full article on https://www.psychologytoday.com/us/blog/wicked-deeds/201806/organized-versus-disorganized-serial-predators

Excerpt
Serial Killers: Modus Operandi, Signature, Staging & Posing
Understanding and classifying serial killer crime scenes. The organized/disorganized classification of offenders is the centerpiece of the F.B.I. profiling approach, and it is explained below.

Organized Offenders

According to the offender and crime scene dichotomy, organized crimes are premeditated and carefully planned, so little evidence is normally found at the scene. Organized criminals, according to the classification scheme, are antisocial (often _psychopathic_) but know right from wrong, are not insane, and show no remorse. Based on historical patterns, organized killers are likely to be above-average intelligent, attractive, married or living with a domestic partner, employed, educated, skilled, orderly, cunning, and controlled. They have some degree of social grace, may even be charming, and often talk and seduce their victims into being captured. With organized offenders, there are typically three separate crime scenes: where the victim was approached by the killer, where the victim was killed, and where the victim's body was disposed of. Organized killers are very difficult to apprehend because they go to inordinate lengths to cover their tracks and often are forensically savvy, meaning they are familiar with police investigation methods. They are likely to follow the news media reports of their crimes and may even correspond with the news media. Ted Bundy, Joel Rifkin, and Dennis Rader are prime examples of organized killers.

Disorganized Offenders

Disorganized crimes, in contrast, are not planned and the criminals typically leave evidence such as fingerprints or blood at the scene of the murder. There is often no attempt to move or otherwise conceal the corpse after the murder. Disorganized criminals may be young, under the influence of alcohol or drugs, or mentally ill. They often have deficient communication and social skills and may be below average in intelligence. The disorganized offender is likely to come from an unstable or dysfunctional family. Disorganized offenders often have been abused physically or sexually by relatives. They are often sexually inhibited, sexually uninformed, and may have sexual aversions or other pathologies. They are more likely than organized criminals to be compulsive masturbators. They are often isolated from others, live alone and are frightened or confused during the commission of their murders. They often do not have reliable transportation, so they kill their victims closer to home than organized offenders. Significantly, disorganized killers will often "blitz" their victims—that is, use sudden and overwhelming force to assault them. The victim's body is usually left where the attack took place, and the killer makes no attempt to hide it. Jack the Ripper is a classic example of the disorganized serial killer. It is also important to note that a serial murder case can also be a mix of organized and disorganized. This occasionally occurs, for example, when there are multiple offenders of different personality types involved in the killings. It can also occur when a lone offender is undergoing a psychological transformation throughout his killing career.
[End of Excerpt.]

What relevance does this have for my aunt's case? I am no expert and obviously not qualified to classify this crime. If I had to give an uneducated guess, I would lean towards the opinion it appears to be more of an organized killing. Coincidentally, the retired detective I spoke of earlier also made this same observation. He stated in the same sentence Ruby had been "shut up" and it appeared to him to be an organized killing. It lines up with the point of having two or three separate locations of the crime. The first location would be the washeteria, the second location being the place where she was killed, and the third location being the place of disposal. Also, the perpetrators taking her clothes and other personal belongings could show someone who is organized in trying to cover up their crime. Ruby had several belongings on her noted by family in the police report as still missing to this day. Ruby's purse, clothes, including undergarments, car keys, eyeglasses, and shoes were never found.

All that was found at the scene of the abduction were the contents described at the laundromat and the items in her car. She had a dishpan and a half full bottle of Wisk soap sitting in the pan on the back seat of her station wagon. That could have been the soap she inquired about on her ride to Charlotte's home and mistakenly overlooked. Like many mothers and grandmothers, Ruby was trying to meet the needs of others and keeping track of even the most mundane things, like making sure to grab the laundry soap.

That small detail brings a touch of sadness to me as I imagine Ruby traveling down the road with her son's young sister-in-law. Doing normal things one does on any normal day. She never could have predicted the abnormal encounter she would face that night at the washeteria.

The details of this case have kept me up at night pondering question after question. Did the killers act in haste, causing the cuts while carelessly cutting her clothes off as to not leave evidence? Or was it a form of sexual mutilation? The case files frustratingly don't answer those questions. The investigators who were working this crime ultimately kept hitting a brick wall. The evidence was less than incriminating; nothing concrete definitively tying anyone to this crime.

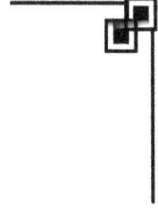

~ CHAPTER EIGHT ~

Whisked Away

S plashed across the front page of the Harding newspaper was the shocking headline: *Body of Missing Professor Found.* Newspapers across the state were reporting on the discovery of Ruby's remains. As the days went by, everyone was still traumatized by this seemingly senseless act. A man by the name of Zell G. Mills came across one of the articles on October 19th about the crime. After reading about her disappearance, it jogged his memory back to the night of October 8th. The police got an unexpected clue when Mr. Mills reported what he had witnessed 11 days before. His eyewitness account opens more intrigue to this already puzzling case.

Recorded on October 20th, this statement from Mr. Mills in Ruby's file was overlooked by me in my first few times going over things. As mentioned, the files were faded and some illegible. I must have overlooked this report due to it being one of the illegible documents needing heavy editing. When I finally deciphered it, my mouth dropped open, and I almost cheered. I was told of this account growing up but never knew if it was real or just a rumor. The way it was told to me sounded like it could have come from an overly excited person with a wild imagination. I was elated this wild tale now seemed credible.

Listed as Supplement #22 in the files.
Furnished by Zell G. Mills, reference two men forcibly removing woman from washeteria.

Zell G. Mills a white male en route to Searcy, AR was interviewed by investigator Paul Blank at Warren on October 19th, 1963. All the following information was learned. Zell Mills is employed by the Caraway chicken processing plant in Warren, AR to transport chickens from Pangburn, AR to Warren, AR. Mills normally makes this trip five nights a week and his route travels through Searcy, AR and follows US 67 route past Harrison's Grocery and the Norge Launderama. On October 8th, 1963, Mills arrived in Searcy between 10:30 p.m. and 11:00 p.m. and traveled through the city onto US 67 S, passing in front of Harrison's Grocery and the Norge Launderama on his right. On this night he observed a white station wagon parked in front of the laundromat, headed into the front wall of that building, in parallel with the north wall of Harrison's Grocery.

He saw another vehicle, described as a dark colored late model automobile, parked in front of the building that joins the Launderama at the north wall and parallel with the east wall of this building. This dark car was parked perpendicular with the front of the vehicle pointing to the right side of the white station wagon.

Mills states that the laundromat was well lit and that the building adjoining it at the north wall was completely dark. Mills observed one man holding a woman by the arm and leading her toward the dark late model car parked in front of the dark building. He said that this woman appeared to be trying to pull back from this man. Mills saw another man following the man and woman and observed that the second man did also have his hands on the woman. All three subjects were outside the laundromat and north of the station wagon and a few feet from the east wall of that establishment. Mills cannot describe the woman, only recalls that both men were wearing dark clothing, possibly suits, and that all three subjects were of the white race.

Mills stated that he actually thought nothing of this at the time. He thought the parties may have been intoxicated, but that he was surprised to read in the papers about the disappearance of the professor and the newspaper account caused him to wonder about the incident. He could not rid the matter from his mind when he learned that the victim had been found. Mills decided to report the incident to Trooper Bill while he was passing through that town later that day.

This statement from Mr. Mills coincides with the statement from the young man, Jack Gardner. Mr. Gardner claimed when he picked up his clothes at 10:50 p.m. the washeteria was vacant. This time frame would make sense and is consistent with the assumption Ruby was abducted shortly before 10:50 p.m. This was proof and validation someone likely saw her being whisked away by not one but two assailants. This statement aligns with what Jerry Bass stated in our conversation. He was adamant about Ruby being abducted and killed by more than one person. Mr. Bass surmised that two people held her by the ankles and arms and hoisted her over into the creek. This validates that assertion.

If Mr. Mills memory serves him correctly, then this could be a huge piece of the puzzle. Now we are talking about two perpetrators, not just one lone killer. This could mean a variety of things. Did two criminals happen to be passing by the launderama where they observed Ruby alone and then tried to rob her? Or worse, violate her? It is not unheard of for two criminals to commit a heinous act on one person but a lot more unlikely. Or were two men hired by an unknown assailant, acting out a hired hit? Were these two men on the lookout for an encounter with Ruby to accomplish what they set out to do?

An alumna from Harding with a hint of sarcasm remarked to me, the two men seen leading Ruby out of the washeteria were obviously from Harding due to their "dark suits." The statement was said in jest but caused me to wonder. Could someone with ties to Harding want this professor dead? Did Ruby know something the public had yet to know?

The idea someone associated with Harding College could somehow be involved in my aunt's murder is unnerving to say the least. There were many people's names associated with Harding that came up in the investigation, which is to be expected because she made her life at Harding, but I did not find anything in the police reports alluding to anyone from Harding faculty being involved in her abduction and murder. As with any unsolved crime, much speculation on who and why this crime was committed has circulated throughout the years with no answers. The remark by the former Harding alumni did make me stop to ponder on why someone would say such a thing.

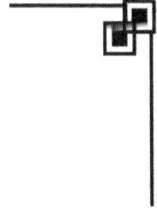

~ CHAPTER NINE ~

Laundry List of Suspects

After the discovery and burial of Ruby's body, investigators were still faced with the hard task of scrutinizing the details of this case. From the information obtained in the police files, it appears as though the detectives were thorough with their inquiries. Many people were interviewed and many given polygraphs.

In reading through the files, I discovered a statement given by an inmate in 1969 that alleges two, or possibly three, Harding students were involved in her murder. While the names and specifics are different than other accounts, the common theory seems to be Ruby knew too much and was killed for her knowledge.

On March 18th, 1969, six years after Ruby's murder, Melvin Lewis Jones gives his statement to Lieutenant Bernard Young. At the time of his statement, Mr. Jones was an inmate, incarcerated in Wilburton, Oklahoma. He was friends with the individuals he suspected, claiming he had firsthand knowledge of who killed Ruby

Stapleton. Below is a summary of Mr. Jones Statement.

Interview of Melbourne Lewis Jones white male date of birth 11/13/36. Presently in custody in Wilburton, Oklahoma. Information requested to be held as confidential. Dictated by Lieutenant Bernard Young, March 19th, 1969.

On March 18th, 1969, Lieutenant Young received information that the above-named subject had some information in reference to a murder that occurred in White County of a schoolteacher. And also, information in reference to another murder that occurred at Bismarck, AR of subject Kent Langston. (to the reader, Langston is printed as Langston in this section of the file but in all other sections it was printed as Laxton) *Telephone check with Lieutenant W.A. Tudor revealed that the murder victim in White County was Frances Stapleton, that she was murdered in White County, that she had gone in a laundromat in Searcy and her car later found still parked at the laundry early next a.m. This being 8th of October 1963 and that the body found on October 19, 1963, about 9 miles South of Searcy. On arrival in Wilburton, Melvin Jones was interviewed, the subject very hard to interview as he talks at random. However, he furnished the following information.*

It is his belief that this subject, Noah Hickman, did kill Mrs. Stapleton, or if he did not, that he has personal knowledge of the crime. That the informant was raised in the Bradford, Demark AR area and that he knows Hickman very well, that Hickman does a lot of drinking, and when the subject is drinking, he does a lot of talking. That Hickman has talked about the murder of Mrs. Stapleton and has described the murder in detail. That the victim did have cotton stuffed in her mouth. He had previously stated to Oklahoma Trooper Crane that the victim also had cotton stuffed in the vagina and rectum. However, he did not state the latter information to this agent. Also, that the victim was mutilated.

Melvin Lewis Jones ultimately stated three names that he thought were involved in Ruby's murder one being Kent Laxton. Jones went on to claim that Kent Laxton was subsequently murdered by Hickman stating, *"That Laxton was getting nervous and was killed by Hickman because he was afraid that he would talk. Informant further advised that at the time of the murder of the teacher that dope was very plentiful on the campus at Harding and that she was instrumental in putting a stop to the dope racket and that persons involved are the ones that had killed her."*

It is a long, confusing story but I would think worth looking into. Again, the claim being, one suspect murdered the other for fear he would "talk." I researched the man's name, and he was found to be murdered/deceased, his time of death matching up to Melvin's account. The details Melvin added regarding the cotton being found in places other than her throat are details not found in any of the other files, which creates more mystery and questions.

Early on during my research, I was in communication with the most recently appointed detective from the Arkansas State Police. He mentioned when he saw the name W.A. Tudor, he felt confident the investigation was at least in good hands back then. Mr. Tudor had a stellar reputation for being direct, thorough, and honest. I saw his name on many documents and noticed he was one of the main investigators working Ruby's case. If only we could talk to him on his thoughts or theories today. W.A. Tudor most likely investigated this claim from the inmate, but there are no records of his findings in Ruby's case file. This is yet another bit of information for a cold case investigator to take on.

As the days wore on, the F.B.I., Arkansas State Police, and investigators continued diligently working to solve this case. Every time I delved into the files, I found more inquiries about possible suspects. There were many memorandums from Detective W.A. Tudor inquiring about multiple criminals all across the US. The police looked at anyone who committed a similar crime and tried to track down their location at the time of the murder. Each inquiry essentially started out the same.

This office is conducting an inquiry into the abduction and murder of Frances Ruby Stapleton, white female of Searcy, Arkansas, who disappeared on Tuesday, October 8th, 1963, and whose decomposed body was found about 15 miles south of Searcy on October 19th, 1963, the victim is the wife of E.R. Stapleton.

The inquiries go on to ask various police departments to investigate certain individuals and their alibis, etc. The investigators were certainly doing their due diligence in seeking out possible suspects.

Many of the suspects investigated were found to have solid alibis, either being incarcerated at the time of the murder or on record of being at work. A lot of dead ends and a lot of unanswered letters were what the police files also held. It is comforting to know though, for the most part, police left no stone unturned. In one inquiry, detectives were trying to corroborate a lead they had, admitting it might be a long shot, but double checking nonetheless. The inquiry states:

Information has been received that two white men; one a teenager and the other an adult, driving a pink Rambler station wagon, bearing a Missouri license plate ET 1922, stopped at a newsstand at North Little Rock yesterday and purchased a Little Rock paper. Both of these subjects in the presence of the newsstand operator hurriedly turned to the article describing the recovery and positive identification of Mrs. Stapleton's body. These men glanced through this article hurriedly and got into their vehicle and left. We realize that these circumstances most probably do not pertain to the abduction or murder of the victim. However, we are simply grasping at straws in an effort to uncover a lead in this matter. Would you please conduct a discreet inquiry of the owner and occupants of the above-described vehicle and ascertain where they were on the night of this abduction. If you suspect there is any connection between these subjects and the crime please contact us collect immediately. If you feel there is no connection, would you notify us of your findings by letter?

As with the many other inquiries, no response was found in Ruby's file relating to this inquiry, but it shows how the investigators were pursuing every avenue in a desperate attempt to solve this crime. I have to wonder if it was a coincidence the people spotted at the news stand drove a pink car, and Ray also drove a pink car. One of the young men he picked up hitchhiking, made the remark to detectives, *"anyone within 5 miles would know he was a homosexual because of what he drove."*

I wonder if these two individuals were acquainted with Ray. Perhaps they were intrigued, not because they were involved in the crime, but because they knew Ray and were merely shocked by the gruesome crime. Sadly, we will never know unless a cold case detective takes this on and discovers more about who the car was registered to. In the files there is a list of Supplements for the case and Supplement #59 is listed as a reply from the Missouri State Police. It stated it was referencing the occupants of the pink Rambler station wagon, but that piece of information was nowhere I could find. It is entirely possible these people were investigated and cleared, and that information is missing from the incomplete files.

There are many people of interest in Ruby's files. One name that remains in circulation is Roger A. Burns, a twenty-two-year-old at the time, U.S. Air Force tech. Burns was convicted of killing Roseann Curran in April 1965, after abducting her by gunpoint from a laundromat. He took Ms. Curran back to his trailer home and while there, shot her in the chest. He stated he wrapped her body in a blanket and left her in a wooded area. He came back the next night and proceeded to mutilate her body.

Burns also tried to kill another young woman, but she was able to escape. Twenty-seven-year-old Mary Kusmer, mother of three, had stopped to use a payphone at a service station where Burns was employed. Burns saw her and stated he was unable to resist the urge to kidnap her and then beat her over the head with a rubber mallet and placed her in the trunk of a car. By a stroke of luck her dress caught in the latch, and she was able to escape.

The circumstances of Ruby's abduction and murder are eerily similar to Burns' victims. Frustratingly, there isn't anything connecting Roger Burns to Ruby's murder; although, in 2014, ASP Special Agent David Moss tried to find out if Burns was stationed near Searcy at the time of Ruby's death. He unfortunately could not find record of Burns being stationed at the missile silo during that time. It is a possible scenario due to the similar crimes but no definitive answers. There are key differences to note about these crimes as well though. One being, Burns was alone when committing these acts, and Mr. Mills reported seeing two assailants taking Ruby out of the washeteria. Another key difference is the manner of violence he chose. Ruby was not shot or hit over the head; she was strangled/suffocated.

Yet again, another interesting inquiry was found in Ruby's file about a young man murdered in Alabama. He had been shot through the forehead in 1973 and left in a wooded area. David Smart was an aerospace engineer for NASA and was reported to be a former student at Harding back in 1963. He was alleged to have been in a sexual relationship with Dr. Stapleton and other men in Searcy. The police in Alabama asked the Arkansas State Police for any information regarding his known acquaintances from 1963 and any contacts he may have had. Including friends, coworkers, employers, landlords, etc. he would have had in Searcy and any same sex relationships he was involved in.

I did not find a follow up letter regarding this man, and it remains a mystery as to why investigators wanted to know his contacts in Searcy at the time of Ruby's death. I tried requesting this man's case file through FOIA, but it appears since it is an unsolved murder, the agency did not have anything to release. I am curious to know who killed this man roughly ten years after Ruby's death, and the motive behind it. What correlation would this crime have to Ruby's murder, if any? The more I read about the secret behavior involving many different people, behind the scenes, I wonder if there was a ring going on, whether with drugs, alcohol, or the sex trade, or all those things.

Unfortunately, the answers to these questions are not in the files. The follow up interviews of all these inquiries are not the only things missing. Sadly, and beyond frustrating, the physical evidence collected on Ruby's case is missing. The physical evidence being: the cotton gag, the piece of belt, the piece of her bra, buttons from her dress, and photographs included on the supplement list. The belt could have been a key piece of evidence.

In a letter from the Deputy State Medical Examiner, Dr. Hoke, he confirmed the brown stains seen on the piece of belt tested positively for blood. Could the perpetrator's blood have been mixed in with Ruby's? Discovering there was blood evidence documented in the file causes me much grief. I know Aunt Ruby suffered immeasurably but knowing there was blood found soaked through her clothing paints the worst picture in my mind as I type this. Another reason I hope this case gets a fresh look and someone is willing to take another shot at unveiling the culprit.

In Ruby's files, it says Agent Moss reached out to the F.B.I. in 2014 to its control unit in Quantico, VA. to see if their agency was storing any physical evidence. In the original case file, it indicates the physical evidence was sent to the F.B.I. for analysis during 1963. Documents show the physical evidence was returned to Arkansas State Police as well. He checked with many departments, and not one of them had any leads on where the evidence could be.

I personally also reached out to several investigators, medical examiners offices, and other departments to try and locate the physical evidence. I was very thankful to one special woman in the medical examiner's office in Little Rock. She tirelessly searched for any answers as to the whereabouts for the items collected in 1963. Unfortunately, the original building that housed evidence from 1963 has since been closed and the contents moved to a new location. I am hopeful the evidence is hiding in a back room waiting to make its debut sooner than later. If DNA could be extracted from the cotton found in her throat and other items, there might be a chance to solve this case.

Even though there is a lack of physical evidence with this crime, there are certainly other things to investigate, and it would be worth someone with the right resources digging deeper into her file. I know a detective could make a professional assessment of the mindset of the killer or killers. I do hope someday someone will take a fresh look at this case and go over the evidence with new eyes.

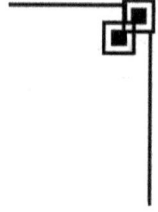

~ Chapter Ten ~

Wrinkled Leads

When you have a loss of this magnitude, it feels like the world should stop, but as we all know, life goes on per usual. Classes and activities resumed at Harding, and Clarita continued dutifully checking for any updates at the police station every so often. The faculty had the task of accommodating the students as well as could be during the grieving process and calming the fear the students must have felt.

As the town and campus were settling in to their new normal, the repetitive cycle of sniffing out leads and coming up empty was still the common thread in this unusual case. The investigators searched high and low for any answers on who would have wanted to commit this heinous act. They tracked down many acquaintances Ray made over the years, while living across country, and could not tie any of them to this crime. They sifted through bank statements, phone records, and administered several polygraphs. All the while coming up empty. I'm not sure what life was like for Ray and Mary Claire, as well as Glen Dewey and his young family, after the dust settled, but Ray continued to reside in Searcy for about a year after the crime.

Strangely again, a violent encounter happened with the Stapleton family, this time the target being Ray, not Ruby. Approximately one year after Ruby's murder, Ray was assaulted by two young men in Searcy. Were these violent encounters connected? This is one of the things mentioned by Clarita to me. It leaves mystery and confusion in the minds of the detectives. The names of the two men are not listed in the files, but the attackers were listed as former students at Harding College. At the time of this assault, they had traveled to Searcy with the purpose of meeting with Ray. The report states the two men roughed up the heavyset professor before rushing back to their hometown, Little Rock. There is much speculation as to their motive.

Were these men vigilantes for Ruby's honor? Much talk around the town was Ruby's husband had been instrumental in her death somehow. Were they listening to idle gossip and then decided to take action to avenge Ruby's death?

Another rumor attached to this assault was the two men were current or former lovers of Ray's from earlier in his years of teaching at Harding, and they accosted him for unknown reasons. Could it be Ray promised them money for sexual services they provided and then not paid them? Were they scorned lovers from their former days at Harding when Ray was a professor there? Or was it possible they were involved in Ruby's death somehow, as in a murder for hire plot against Professor Ruby, and wanted their payout? That might seem farfetched, but every angle needs to be scrutinized.

The only information in the files about the assault states that the two were arrested, and when it was time for them to be tried, Ray skipped town with his daughter Mary Claire and never went back to Searcy. Without Ray as a witness, the men could not be tried. The obvious question on everyone's mind was, why would Ray skip town if the criminals were identified and most likely about to be convicted? Did he leave due to fear, or was he leaving due to guilt in some way? Was he afraid if he testified against them, they might spill the beans about something he had done? Without evidence linking anything to the crime, it is only speculation.

Unfortunately, I don't think we will ever know what the men's motives were, just like the unknown motives for the two men that broke into Ruby's home. Was it possible they were the same men? It is surprising to me there is not more information about the break in and the attack on Ray in the police files. The cycle of dead ends continued even though there was countless information in the files.

◈◈

Another interesting piece of the puzzle, which could be another possible lead, was something I found buried deep within the files. I couldn't fight the feeling this document was hidden away. It certainly created a quandary of questions. The item was a twenty-one-page letter written in cursive and then xeroxed onto paper. Like many of the documents in Ruby's case file, it was faded, with many words being unreadable. The page numbers were faded, some even running off the page, which made putting this letter in order rather difficult. A sure deterrent for someone wanting to restore this lengthy, swirly penned document. Fortunately, giving up is not in my nature and so began my months long work of restoring this piece of information. I was able to date this letter as being written in approximately 1993.

I am hesitant to print the letter word for word in its entirety, but I will do my best to explain the contents. Again, I want to provide all information that could be helpful to the case. In the early 1990s, a woman had reason to suspect her estranged husband might know something about Ruby's murder. This woman confided in a mentor type friend; the friend I will call by an alias, "Vivian." Vivian then reported this information to a detective, stating she could not rest if she did not report the information she was told.

Mysteriously, Vivian referred to the woman who confided in her, and this woman's husband, by initials only. From the tone of the letter, I can assume the detective knew who she was referring to, and she didn't want to put the names in writing for safety reasons. As usual, my curiosity was piqued, and I became intent on discovering who this unnamed woman was. Yet again, my daughter Aryanna stepped in as lead investigator and got to work tracking down the identities of those in question. Armed with the initials and a random picture of a torn note with a name scrawled at the bottom, in the back of Ruby's file, she went to the internet. Miraculously, after much research and putting things/names together in her mind, she tracked down the complete names of the individuals in question. It is amazing what young people can do in this age of technology. I think Aryanna would have made a great code breaker back in the day.

I must admit, I did not have much hope even though Aryanna provided me a name. Taking the name of the woman, I did some digging myself and found who I thought to be a relative of this woman. I reached out in January 2024, and much to my surprise this person was the woman in question's daughter and was willing to chat with me. I've decided to keep the anonymity going and will be referring to the woman that confided in Vivian as Matilda. Again, these are not the names or initials given in the letter.

The Contents in the Letter Addressed to a Detective.

Matilda states several reasons as to why she suspects her husband of some involvement. Matilda's husband was known to be violent and was abusive towards Matilda, known to have many affairs, and he, being a very young man in 1963, had an affinity for much older women. He was even rumored to have forced himself upon an older woman. He also threatened his now estranged wife on numerous occasions. He would make ominous statements saying she could end up like the teacher or end up dead from suicide. This individual used fear to control his wife, and she was very afraid to report anything to police.

Another reason why Matilda considered her husband a suspect was the proximity between his place of employment and the place of abduction. The suspected man also lived and previously worked near the place of discovery of Ruby's body near Beebe. Shortly before the murder, he took another a job at a place of business near the washeteria. This man was also known to always carry a cotton rag and had easy access to the type of cotton found in Ruby's throat, through his place of employment. Ironically enough, he was also known to be in communication with Ruby through services performed at his place of employment many times prior to Ruby's death. Ruby and her family attended the same church as this man and his family. I want to clarify that while Ruby knew of this man through church and his work, Ruby and this man had no known relationship outside of these minor exchanges during business hours.

Matilda could not remember the year her husband worked at the business near the location where the body was left but had come across a picture of her husband with their newborn baby (this baby, now grown, would end up being the relative I tracked down and contacted). The baby was born in June of 1963, and the man in question had on a uniform clearly showing his employment at the place near Bull Creek. Matilda felt she had hit pay dirt. She now had proof her husband had been employed near the place Ruby was dumped although her memory was still hazy.

Matilda asked to be driven to the place of discovery to jog her memory. She wanted to know exactly how far away the discovery site was from her husband's then place of employment. She knew in the early '60s she and her husband also lived near Beebe but didn't know the exact place the body was found, so she wanted to find the spot and compare the distance. The two women, Vivian, and Matilda (why do I want to give them nicknames and call them Viv and Maddie? I have a vision of two women, soul sisters on a valiant crusade, stopping at nothing for the sake of justice.) Along with another roped in crusader, they took the drive out to Bull Creek from Searcy to search for the place of discovery.

Vivian states Matilda had a sense of urgency about her as she searched the roads she formerly traveled. As the three searchers neared the suspected area of discovery, they came to a slow roll down a dirt road and happened upon a man standing in his driveway. As luck, or fate, would have it, the man turned out to be Jerry Bass Sr. They pulled over and stated they were investigating a cold case about a professor and inquired, did this man have any idea where the body was found? The man replied to the astonishment of the trio, "Ma'am, my son was the one who found the body."

Jerry Bass Sr. took the group over to the place of discovery off Apple Road along Bull Creek. Matilda confirmed her former residence and husband's former place of employment were indeed a stone's throw from where Ruby was so heinously dumped. The trio saw what they wanted and headed back to Searcy, all in quiet contemplation. Vivian states in the letter neither her nor Matilda could convince themselves Matilda's husband was not involved.

Vivian, the author of the letter, has since passed away, but using my daughter's bloodhound skills, we eventually tracked down Vivian's daughter in September 2023. I told her who I was and my reason for contacting her. Another time where I was beyond grateful for another stranger's willingness to connect me to the past. I told her how I had come across the letter, and although she did not know the specifics in her mother's letter, she confirmed she had heard rumblings of someone's husband confessing on a death bed or in a state of delirium due to fever. She said her mother was a bit kooky but certainly had her wits about her and would only be providing this type of information to law enforcement to aid in solving the crime.

At the time of Ruby's death, Matilda was a very young mother in the throes of raising children and making ends meet on a small income. Those years were spent keeping the peace between her and her husband for her children's sake. In those days, women often overlooked a hard situation, no matter how terrible. Again, probably for the same reason Ruby and Ray stayed married. This young family in the 1960s attended the church of Christ, just like Ruby and her family. Divorce was looked down upon by the church even when there might be a very good reason to end the union.

Years later, when this letter was written and deposited to the police, Matilda was going through a divorce that had been years in the making. Finally having the courage and financial standing to leave, she went through with the divorce and put that part of life behind her. In seeking counsel during divorce proceedings, she confided in a mentor from church. This mentor, Vivian, couldn't keep this information to herself. Knowing about the death of Professor Ruby Stapleton, she too wanted this murder solved, and if there was even a slight chance what this woman was telling her was true, she wanted it known to law enforcement.

In my talks with Matilda's family, it was clear this lead could be a very good one. Matilda's daughter stated to me she has been estranged from her father for thirty years for personal reasons but didn't think he was capable of a crime so heinous.

Although Matilda's hunch about her husband could be a bit off, there potentially could be vital information her husband knew in relation to the crime. Even if it was a small detail like him knowing who else had a business relationship with Ruby through his place of employment. I think he could be a source of information even if he is not the culprit. This man is alive and would be someone of interest to talk to.

I came across an email addressed to the detective who received this letter back in 1993. The detective on the case in 2014 was inquiring as to why the people in the letter were not investigated. The detective stated that he thought the woman Vivian was a little off the wall and did not take this claim seriously. It sure seems like a lot of trouble to go to for a woman just to be reporting a story that had no merit. Even if this turns out to be nothing, it could also turn out to be everything. Why not follow it to the end? I have yet to discuss anything about this information with law enforcement.

The letter closes with Vivian noting how this crime has affected the family of Ruby Stapleton.

This whole group of people seem to be haunted by this 30-year-old event. I do not wish to cause trouble for anyone, but I do not know how I can sleep at night if I do not give the account to you. You are trained for making judgements about these matters. As for myself, all I need is to know you did read this report.

Well, "Vivian," I've read this report, and I am grateful for your courage.

◈◈

One last thing I want to include about this letter from Vivian was an interesting story she heard while crusading through Bull Creek. Vivian stated Jerry Bass Sr. shared with the three crusaders that day a story from the day of discovery long ago. He stated that before investigators identified the remains as Ruby's, a man by the name of L.C. Sears came out to Bull creek wanting to see for himself where Ruby was left. L.C. Sears worked in the same department as Ruby and later went on to become the Dean of students at Harding. Jerry Bass Sr. claimed this man crawled down the embankment and said if he could see some hair, he would undoubtedly know it was the missing professor. He didn't want to wait on dental records.

Ruby was loved and respected by many, and people wanted answers. The story continued, stating L.C. Sears indeed found some black hair left behind in the debris pile and stated, "It was her alright." I was not able to validate or disprove this claim, but I wanted to include this portion of the letter. It seems like a plausible story and one that Jerry Bass Sr. would not pull out of thin air. This crime is far reaching, and I imagine there were many people handling this trauma with an aggressive pursuit of justice.

Perhaps we will never get answers as to the validity of all these claims and stories in this letter, but I hope it is honoring to Vivian's quest for justice and hopefully will cause more talk on this case.

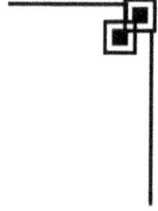

~ CHAPTER ELEVEN ~

The Scent of Reflection

The murmurings on this case today are as silent as the dryers left by Ruby Stapleton on that October night, long ago. While you may still hear whispers of speculation among longtime residents of Searcy, echoes of this case are slowly fading away. According to the Arkansas State Police, this case is considered a closed one. As time passes, memories fade, and few people remain with ties to this story. While it might appear, there is little chance of this crime being solved, there is hope a fresh look will be given to this case by a detective or even a super sleuth like me. It is not unheard of for crimes decades old to be solved.

I believe with certainty the answer to this puzzle is buried deep within the worn, faded files of this case, and it is entirely possible to solve this crime. The world of DNA is a magical one, with many criminals being brought to justice by DNA alone. There are countless stories of bodies being exhumed and suspects being convicted, as well as exonerated. According to science, fingernails can last up to a thousand years, depending on the environmental conditions. Could trace DNA be found from exhuming Ruby from her place of rest? It could be worthwhile to exhume Ruby and see what the findings would be. We will never know unless it is done.

❖❖

A common opinion about this crime is that it was a planned abduction and murder. On the other side of opinion, some believe the crime was random. The lateness of the hour, and the somewhat remoteness of the location of the washeteria, could likely point to a crime of opportunity. Overall, no matter which side of opinion you are on, the lingering question in everyone's mind is, will this simple, quiet professor's murder ever be solved?

❖❖

In summary, here are the known facts as well as important observations of this case.

- Ruby Stapleton was kidnapped and murdered on the night of October 8th, 1963, most likely by two men, according to the eyewitness account of seeing two assailants leading Ruby out of the Norge Launderama/washeteria.
- The eyewitness account of an unusually upset and distracted professor at a stop-sign on the day of her abduction.
- She was known in the public eye to be wealthy, having inherited land, and had recently received a large profit from Harding from selling her personal properties.
- Two unknown perpetrators broke into her home for unknown reasons shortly before her murder.
- Ray had secrets that cost him his job at Harding, jeopardized other jobs, and secrets that could cause him jailtime.
- Ray did not have free access to all of Ruby's wealth.
- Ray spoke of wanting to divorce Ruby to more than one person shortly before the crime.

- Ray expressed fear for Ruby due to his involvement with criminal activity and concern that people knew he was worth more without her in the picture.
- Ray was being threatened and blackmailed, which could inadvertently put Ruby in danger.
- Ruby was very upset by the alcohol and drugs running rampant on Harding campus in the early '60s and had made it her mission to put a stop to it.
- Ruby was dealing with serious, secret personal issues regarding her marriage.
- Ruby was alone at the washeteria and a perfect victim for a sexual predator or thief to commit a crime of opportunity.

Below is a summary of observations that give credit to the possibility Ruby was being followed or watched, which in turn points to a premediated abduction.

- Clarita and other bystander's reports of a dark colored sedan circling Ruby's house and Harding campus the day of the abduction. The description of the sedan also ironically matches the description of the car idling outside of Ruby's home prior to her disappearance and the car seen at the washeteria on October 8th.
- The observation of Ruby staring out the window on the day of her abduction, seeming nervous and distracted prior to her disappearance.
- Jerry Bass' opinion that two people were needed to put her body in the creek. Two offenders point to a planned event.

In the aftermath the community of Searcy grappled with the outcome and reflected on the unknown issues that allowed such a crime to unfold. Ruby's story is full of mystery and leaves a trail of emptiness and bewilderment. The stories of grief, courage, and resilience that come after a loss such as Ruby's deserve their own spotlight. I have to say witnessing firsthand what crime does to a family, I am encouraged by the survivors. Ruby's immediate family and extended family has been forced to move on, putting one foot in front of the other, propelling forward, albeit sometimes robotically.

Five short years after Ruby was murdered, Ray Stapleton passed away at his home in Kansas. I was told he died of natural causes. What happened after he died was not natural at all.

As I was contemplating how to include this unusual tidbit in my book, I happened to be at a scheduled hair appointment. I had brought my laptop with me to work on my book while I waited for my color to process. I've worked on this book in many places. The dreaded car line to pick up my 2nd and 8th graders from school, the parking lot of a grocery store, a doctor's office waiting room, hotel rooms, bubble baths, and most often, locked in my bedroom away from interruptions. On the day my miracle worker, Heather, was bringing my dull blonde hair back to its shining glory, I recalled this unusual story. I think we can all agree our hairdresser often knows more about us than our own family. Heather was one of the first people I shared with about my plan to write about my aunt Ruby, and she has supported me every step of the way. On the day of my appointment, I quickly told her the tidbit about Ray, and the comments began. Her assistant was within earshot and added her thoughts as well. "Well, if that's not poetic justice." "Karma is the universe's way of saying checkmate!" "He got what he deserved!"

The piece of info they were reacting to with such feeling was the condition in which his body was found.

Ray was not found right away, and his body was in an advanced state of decomposition, much like Ruby's was at the time of her recovery.

His pet cats were naturally hungry as the days wore on and no one was there to feed them. I think you can guess what I am about to write. When Ray Stapleton was found, his hands and other parts of his body had been eaten by his cats. I shudder at the thought. I am not one to wholeheartedly believe in "Karma," but I do believe in the sentiment, what goes around comes around.

That's not to say I believe Ray was guilty. I believe the guilty person is for the investigators to figure out. I do believe Ray was guilty of the crime of being a sexual predator. I feel a catch in my heart when I think about the past victims he preyed upon. I think the way he used money as an incentive for someone to commit acts they wouldn't normally commit was a devious way of manipulating vulnerable people.

This book was written to state the facts obtained through my

FOIA request and to help investigators along in researching this case. Not to influence anyone to believe if someone was guilty or not guilty. The reader can come up with their own theories, and I hope I have shared facts that are helpful in solving this long-standing mystery.

~ CHAPTER TWELVE ~

Wash. Rinse. Repeat: The Cycle of Life

As this book nears the end, I sit contemplating the ripple effects that resonate long after a case is closed. Glen Dewey and his wife Pat chose to stay out of the spotlight and retreat in the best way they knew how. I witnessed firsthand just how much they want out of the circus and still desire anonymity to this day. I wanted to provide an opportunity for them to speak out if they were inclined to do so and visited them on a whim. My trusty little side kick, Aryanna, was by my side again as we walked with nervous anticipation up to Glen Dewey's door. In my defense, I would have preferred to call beforehand, but theirs is a private number.

As we approached the house, we noticed a sign posted on the door with faded, curling edges. The sign reads: no visitors or solicitors of any kind. It looked to have been placed on the door quite some time ago. I hesitated out of respect but then remembered when my mother visited them years before, in the same type of fashion, stopping by unannounced. She and Glen Dewey ended up having a productive conversation. I thought maybe because we are family, an unplanned visit would be okay, so I lightly knocked on the door. I was wrong. Pat and Glen Dewey declined a chance to comment and respectfully asked me to leave their porch. I respected their wishes. I do not want to disturb their peace. I just want my Aunt Ruby's crime solved, and I am aware digging into the past, bringing things to light, might evoke a bit of unease in some. It is a battle of feelings as I navigate this path of wanting to expose the perpetrator responsible for Ruby's death but wanting to protect the family at the same time.

We turned to walk back to our car, and my daughter said, "Mom, this could be their only chance to say something, we should go back and try once more, for their sake." I admire my daughter's tenacity for truth seeking and truth sharing. I do know she and I both wish to provide details from the immediate family that could possibly help solve this crime. But I saw the tormented look in my much older cousin's eyes, and I think the right decision was to let it go. We walked back to our car that day reminded again of just how devastating this crime has been. I can only imagine the trauma and invasive eyes on Ruby's immediate family for so long. I wish them peace and rest.

Ultimately, this true crime story serves as a sobering reminder that behind every case lies a web of complexity urging us to remain vigilant in our pursuit of justice and compassion. The end of this book is not the end of the story. This story challenges us to confront the darker aspects of our nature while highlighting the unwavering determination of those who strive to bring light to the shadows. I hope this book brings this case out of the shadows and into the light.

The lot that once held the washeteria is now empty; the remnants of the previous building outline the crumbling pavement. The building may be gone, but the mystery remains. The last chapter of this manuscript is completed, but the memories linger. The journey for justice continues, and I complete this book with so many questions. I wonder, was and is everything being done to solve this case? This book is my contribution to the journey that awaits, the journey of solving this mystery.

One more footnote I want to include in this story. As I climbed into my SUV after spending the afternoon on Harding campus, I instinctively turned on the radio. When the song "Ruby Tuesday" by The Rolling Stones started flowing through the speakers, I wasn't even surprised. I just shook my head and said of course! Thinking about my aunt going missing on a mundane Tuesday night, all those years ago, just a short drive from where I was sitting in my car, made me realize how unexpected life is and the roads we travel are not always what we anticipate.

I pulled away from Searcy, listening to Goodbye Ruby Tuesday with a stillness in my soul. What a treasure to live and breathe and experience life with all the bad, good, and everything in between. As the final page turns, may the echoes of this story resonate within you.

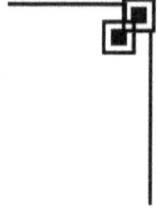

~ EPILOGUE ~

This journey has taken me many places and introduced me to many special people. Naturally, one place I found myself drawn to was Harding University. As I walked across campus after one of my meetings with the library's archivist, I was reminded of previous visits at a time when I was much younger. I remember trying out the infamous white swings scattered across the manicured lawn. The swings have become a resting point for thousands of students throughout the years. In the 1940s the college kept stringent rules for doting couples. The courting pairs were encouraged to stay in groups of six while walking throughout the campus and were only allowed in cars together with special permission. But much to their delight, they were permitted to sit on the swings with one rule: not after dark. Nowadays, outdoor lights have been installed and rules have been lifted. Anyone can sit on the swings whenever they please, as long as it's not between the hours of 1 a.m. to 5 a.m. Harding has seen its share of changes, many being changes for the good of society, and the swings are a constant reminder of the rich history of Harding University.

Another memory I had while visiting Harding was viewing the special bricks laid in memory of previous students and faculty. The bricks honored those that were a part of this close-knit community. Although I have visited Harding campus several times, I hadn't viewed the bricks in over 20 years. I could hardly remember where my family's bricks were located. I carefully walked along the bumpy brick path, my feet bare from the pain of walking in heels on a cobblestone like sidewalk. For a moment, I did not care what the students milling around the campus thought of me and my bare feet. For a moment, I was turning an ordinary walk into a captivating quest for a piece of hidden significance. Here I was, strolling leisurely along, heels swaying in one hand, my eyes keenly scanning the ground as I searched for Ruby's name. Each step I took resonated with echoes of the past as I sought out the elusive bricks. The sound of my feet treading lightly on the ground mingled with the subtle whispers of history. I finally spotted the bricks with familiar names imprinted to stand the test of time. They are located between the front lawn and the bell tower, with, ironically, the American Heritage building overseeing their special spot.

I murmured their names and relation out loud as my eyes scanned the path, "*B. Frank Lowery...great great grandpa...Ruth Lowery Sanner...great grandma...Reuben Lincoln Sanner...great grandpa...Rose Marie Lowery...sister to Ruby...Helen Sanner Hogins...grandma...Raymond Buel Hogins...granddad...Lillian Sanner Lowery...another sister.*"

And then my eyes were drawn to one lone, brightly colored green leaf resting on the corner of a brick. The cobblestone path was clear of any debris except this one spot. The brick was a bit off to the side, placed away from the others. I whispered with an already knowing smile, "*Ruby Lowery Stapleton.*"

The sight of Ruby's brick so blatantly marked with a leaf was not lost on me. This final display of serendipity shows me once again we do not know everything about the unseen. I felt a peace in my spirit as I pondered the significance of this experience. I stood under the sweeping oaks lining the campus, my gaze looking up through the fluttering trees as their leaves danced with a small gust of wind passing through. I could see the clouds silently floating by, surrounded by a bright blue sky. I felt in that moment that all was right with the world, and I was exactly where I was supposed to be and doing exactly what I was called to do. I looked back down at the brick I had undoubtedly been led to and reminisced on my decision to embark on this quest. I had no idea the challenges I would face or the clarity I would gain. I didn't anticipate the elation felt after each chapter was completed, as if I had just reached another milestone bringing me closer to my goal. My goal has always been transparency and sharing truths. I want this penned narrative to resonate with family and readers for years to come. I want the family to have knowledge not previously known.

I felt a sense of Ruby's spirit that day at Harding. Everything had come full circle. Too many coincidences and happenings cannot be ignored. As I think of all the places of importance to this case and Ruby herself, I ponder as to why there are no memorials. Few today walk by her painting in the library knowing her story. One might have a fleeting thought that someone's grandma is being honored with a picture if they even have a thought at all.

As I documented the ironic happening while locating her brick that day with a few pictures, I wrapped up my time at the University that Ruby had loved so much. This was her legacy. The time she spent making Harding University what it is today, the properties she gave up for the campus to grow, the many years of teaching, the relationships forged with students, the respect and admiration of her cohorts, the commitment to her faith even when it was hard, the fight to hold on to something she believed in, even in turbulent times: this was Ruby Stapleton. Ruby's legacy lives on, and her life was not in vain. She was taken out of this world in a wrong, inhumane way but that does not change who she was and what she should be remembered for. Ruby's legacy was built upon a foundation of resilience, her love of education, a determination to forge ahead in tough times, and her unwavering commitment to making a difference in the lives of others. Ruby's legacy leaves a lasting imprint on the hearts and minds of those she touched.

Ruby's memory brick at Harding University. Note the leaf in the upper left corner

❖

One-year-old Frances Ruby Lowery

1926

Ruby as "Best All Around Girl" in a lovely, embroidered blouse

Ruby as a young child, pictured with her family. Father-Benjamin Franklin Lowery, Sisters: (top) Rose Marie, Ruth: (bottom) Lillian and Ruby Mother-Clara Isabelle

LOWERY FAMILY
Lillian, Franklin, Florence, B. Frank, Clara, Ruby, Marie, Ruth

Ruby and Ray standing behind friends on a swing at Harding

Ray and Ruby in their younger years, admiring goldfish while in Little Rock

Ruby and Ray with their children Glen Dewey and Mary Claire

Ruby and Glen Dewey as a 4-year-old
A moment capturing the bond between mother and son.

Ray with his children, Glen Dewey and Mary Claire

Helen Sanner-Hogins (my grandma) with her cousins, Glen Dewey
and Mary Claire

Front three: Mary Claire holding dog, Betty and Clarita Bartley
in matching dresses. Behind: Florence, Ruth, Ruby, B. Frank,
Helen holding her daughter Sherilyn

Clarita with friend on Harding campus 1963

Clarita Bartley Petit Jean Yearbook Photo 1962-1963

Mary Claire Stapleton Petit Jean Yearbook Photo 1961-1962

Mary Claire Stapleton

BIRTHS

Nancy Jill, to Mr. and Mrs. Neil B. Cope of 1043 Chicago, Evanston, Illinois, on September 17. Mr. Cope is working on the staff of the Chicago Tribune.

Clarita Dorothea, to Mr. and Mrs. J. E. Bartley, Jr., on August 27. The Bartleys are teaching at Joiner, Arkansas.

Mary Claire to Mr. and Mrs. E. R. Stapleton on September 7 at Searcy. The Stapletons are members of the Harding faculty.

Clarita and Mary Claire's birth announcements in the Harding Bulletin

BEST ALL-AROUND GIRL.

"All Around Girl"

FRANCES RUBY LOWERY
Seventh Grade
"I'll do that next summer."

Ruby's faculty picture, when as a student, she taught 7th grade Math.

FRANCES RUBY LOWERY

Ruby as College Grad 1926

Frances Ruby Lowery, A.B.

Davenport, Nebraska

Major: English.

Harper College, '22-'24; Business Manager, *The Angelos*, '22-'23; Editor, *The Angelos*, '23-'24; Harding College, '24-'26; Teacher in Training School, '24-'26; Best All-Round Girl, '24-'25, '25-'26; Assistant Editor, PETIT JEAN, '24-'25; Editor, PETIT JEAN, '25-'26.

"POKEY"

Being full of the ideals and interests of the school when she finished two years of work at Harper College, she came to Harding, and has faithfully lived up to its ideals and worked for its interests since its very beginning. She is a born leader in any activity in which she engages, and is always giving up personal preferences and sometimes slighting her own work that she may help others. Her time is not her own; she lives for others—that is why she was chosen the best all-round girl; the favorite chaperon on pleasure trips, the confidant of those in need of sympathy or advice, a teacher in the training school who enjoys profound respect and affection of all who are or have been her pupils. Every one loves her, especially Freshmen; for though but a student teacher, both Freshmen academy and college classes have chosen her as Sponsor. As Assistant Editor of the PETIT JEAN last year and as Editor in Chief this year, she has done a work for which she is due much credit. These are a few of the many things we think of in connection with her.

28

Frances Ruby Lowery, B.A.

Ruby 1927 Faculty Photo

Faculty picture Ruby

Ray and Ruby pictured in Petit Jean yearbook as faculty

ROSE MARIE LOWERY

B. A. Spanish Major

DAVENPORT, NEBRASKA

Ruby's sister Rose Marie that passed away due to illness at 30

Rose Marie taught Art at Harding and was a very talented painter

The poem at the bottom of the pic above:
As long as lovely flowers grow
May their sweet fragrance with you go
To tell, in just their simple way,
The wish and cheer I send today
                    Rose Marie 1929

Paintings by Rose Marie. Hanging in my mother's house today

Ruby seated on far right with pen in hand. Petit Jean Yearbook staff

Petit Jean Yearbook Faculty photo 1960

Ruby in Yearbook Faculty Photo 1961

CLARITA FLORENCE LOWERY, *Davenport, Neb.*

Candidate for B. A. Degree

Major: *English*

Ju-Go-Ju '30, '31, '33, '39; Vice-President Ju-Go-
Ju '33, President '39; Dramatic Club, '30, '31, '33;
Campus Players '31, '33; Mixed Chorus '30; Glee
Club '30, Trailmakers '31; Pep Squad '31; Press
Club '30, '31, '33; Editor Bison '31, '33; Petit Jean
Staff '31, '33; Petit Jean Artist '33; Poetry Club
'39; Arkansas Club '39.

*"Good manners and soft words have brought
many a difficult thing to pass."*

Ruby's sister Florence (Clarita's Mother)

62

Mrs. E. R. Stapleton
B.A., M.A.

English

Ruby as faculty

Beautiful Ruby pictured in beautiful braids. Petit Jean Yearbook faculty

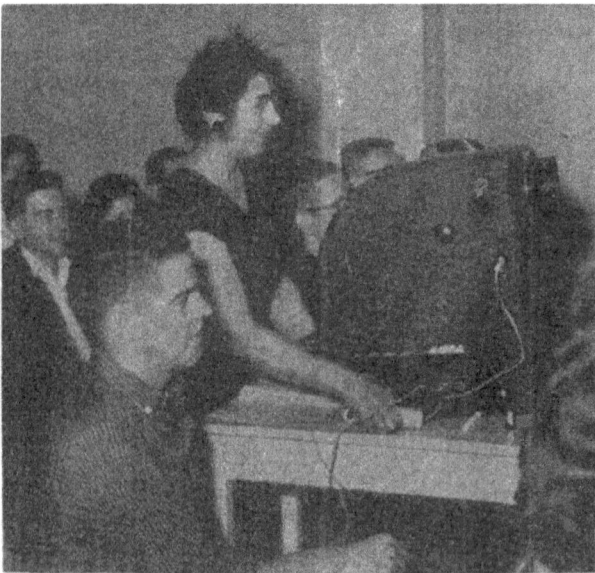

MRS. R. L. STAPLETON used many devices to make her English classes interesting for her students.

Ruby in her element

Dedicated to . . .

Dr. E. R. STAPLETON

. . . in tribute to him for his long service and sincere interest in Harding College, for his faith in the ability and character of youth, for his enthusiasm and friendliness toward all of us, for his faithful Christian life and the example he has been to us who have known him.

Dedication To Ray in the 1948-1949 Petit Jean Yearbook

E.R. Stapleton faculty picture, 1944 Petit Jean Harding Yearbook

E. R. Stapleton
B.A., M.C.E., Ph.D.

Business Administration

Ray at he and Ruby's first home, 904 E. Center Street. Glen Dewey later sold this property to Harding

George S. Benson

Marguerite O'Banion, secretary of George S. Benson. Miss Obanion and Mr. Benson married in 1983, after the death of his wife

134

GEORGE S. BENSON
President
B.A. B.S. M.A. LL.D

THE ADMINISTRATION

George S. Benson

Newspaper ads from the 1960s

Norge Ad

City and Brookshire tire shops robbed 10/8/63 next to Norge Launderama

Grocery adjacent to Norge Launderama

FROSTY TREAT

Take a study break — go to the FROSTY TREAT
and treat yourself to a thick malt
and a juicy hamburger.

David B. Burks
American Heritage

Since it was dedicated in 1965, the Burks American Heritage building has been a major hub on campus. Originally called the American Heritage/Alumni Building, it houses a cafeteria, hotel, meeting rooms, and administrative offices. A renovation in 2006 added Cone Chapel. Following president David Burks' retirement in 2013, the board of trustees renamed the building the David B. Burks American Heritage Building.

1965

Building where Ruby's houses once stood

Special SA Edition

The Harding BISON

Welcome New Students

VOLUME XXXVIII, NUMBER 1   HARDING COLLEGE, SEARCY, ARKANSAS   SEPTEMBER 13, 1963

Plans Completed For Construction

Construction has virtually begun on Harding College's new American heritage center and alumni building.

"As soon as grading and leveling are finished, the actual construction will begin, probably in a week or two," stated President George S. Benson. "The target date for completion is slated for August, 1964," he added.

Largest Building

The building will be the largest, most attractive, and offer the widest variety of services of all the structures on campus. It completes the quadrangle of buildings with the main campus as its center.

Clearing the way for the $700,000 structure has involved the razing of four houses and the moving of three others.

The four adjacent properties north of the campus were purchased from Dr. and Mrs. E. R. Stapleton for the building location. Two other properties were bought on Market Street to allow for an entrance and parking space for the building.

Other Buildings Authorized

Other buildings authorized by the Harding Board for beginning of construction this year are a recording studio and concert hall to be built behind the music building, the new library on the campus of the Graduate School of Bible and Religion in Memphis and the first of two Memphis apartment buildings for married students.

In addition, President George S. Benson recently announced the purchase of Hawkins Clinic Hospital, its parking lot and some adjacent L. C. Sears property south of the hospital.

l Conference

Searcy Gripped by Mystery

HUSBAND, DAUGHTER, SON WAIT PATIENTLY — English professor (inset) missing since Tuesday

Donna Axum to Perform With Orchestra Society

RUFUS MORGAN

Savings Group Picks Morgan

DONNA AXUM — Slated to sing

Morrilton Fisherman Drowns

Mary Claire, Glen Dewey, and Ray appear in newspaper

140

"Scene of Disappearance-pictured above is the washeteria on South Main St. from which Mrs. E.R. Stapleton disappeared Tuesday night. It is located in the same area in which two Searcy business firms were broken into the same night."

Suspect Roger Burns with victim Roseann Curran in center

Coroner Allen Foster out front of Norge Launderama

American Heritage Building next to Ruby's home on Harding campus

Harding College 1963

Harding campus 1960s. The route the dark car would have taken. Ruby's house was located on Center Street

An aerial view of the foundations where the grocery store, washeteria and pest control building once stood

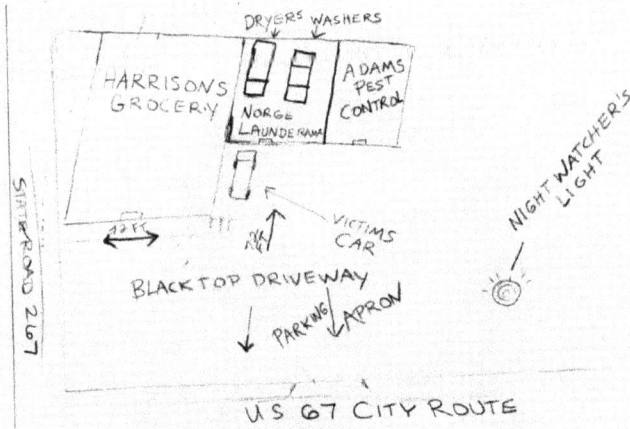

Scene of abduction at Norge Launderama as drawn in Ruby's case file. Retraced and darkened for clarity

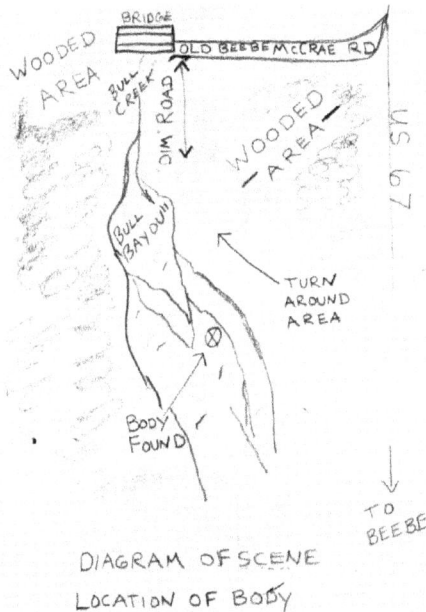

Area where body was found as drawn in Ruby's case file.
Retraced and darkened for clarity

1904   Ruby Lowery Stapleton   1965

In Memoriam

For more than thirty years Ruby Lowery Stapleton gave dedicated and unselfish service to Harding College. The only graduate of the class of 1926, she was a leader in campus activities and a superior student academically. After completing the M.A. degree at the University of Oklahoma, she returned to Harding in 1932 to teach English and journalism and to sponsor the student publications. When the college moved from Morrilton to Searcy in the summer of 1934, she supervised the moving of furniture and other facilities. Mrs. Stapleton was dedicated to the cause of Christ and to Christian education. Her friendly smile and genuine interest in students influenced for good thousands of lives. A memorial service was held in the College Auditorium on October 23rd. She is survived by her husband, Dr. E.R. Stapleton, a son, Glen Dewey, and a daughter Mary Claire, a senior home economics major.

Jerry Bass and me at place of discovery

Straining to see beyond the branches. To be in the place
Ruby was left was surreal

A large bee took a liking to my hair, and I was shooing it away frantically. Mr.
Bass chided with a chuckle, 'You think that bees involved in the murder?'

Harding College at Morrilton, AR

Harding University Today

Me and Hannah Wood, Harding Library's Archivist

Ruby's memorial that hangs at Harding's Brackett Library

MRS. RUBY LOWERY STAPLETON

FEBRUARY 27, 1904 - OCTOBER 8, 1963

A GRADUATE OF THE COLLEGE IN 1926.
SHE BEGAN TEACHING AT HARDING IN
1932. HERS WAS A QUIET LIFE, A
LIFE OF DEDICATION AND SERVICE.

Beneath Ruby's memorial

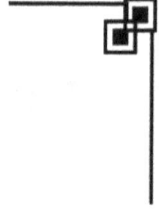

~ THE STATEMENTS ~

The following statements I received through my FOIA request to the Arkansas State Police shed light on the personal relationships Ruby had. I have also included a variety of statements and inquiries to show the diligence of investigators while they worked to solve this case.

While some of these statements may not bring the suspect closer to apprehension, it is important to take into consideration all the evidence documented in the files. I want to preface a warning as some of these statements are graphic in nature and might be shocking to read.

Further contributing to the ambiguity of this case are the lack of comments and questions from investigators in these statements. We do not know their line of questioning and if the interviewers might have elicited certain responses. These statements look like one long monologue, but in fact there were probably pauses and questions from detectives.

In the statements, you can clearly see the Stapleton family had issues. That's not to say they would want harm to come to each other. Like most families, they had their ups and downs, but that's common in life. With an array of personalities and our complex human nature, many times we have strife with the people we cherish the most. I know without a doubt Ruby loved her family, and her family loved her. Even with their minor rifts and disagreements.

The first statement I am including is from Ruby's daughter, Mary Claire Stapleton.

It is evident there was tension between mother and daughter.

Keep in mind, often in moments under duress, things are presented in a more negative light. It was day six of Ruby's disappearance when this interview was conducted, and emotions were at an all-time high. I felt Mary Claire's sentiment though part of her statement was somewhat relatable. Aryanna, my 20-year-old daughter at the time of this writing, recently moved home for a short stretch. We are the best of friends, but when she moved out, we both breathed a sigh of relief. I think we can all agree when our children go from childhood to adulthood, sometimes parents have trouble realizing their baby is not a baby anymore. The now grown child does not want to be treated as a minor, and sometimes tension ensues.

I have put myself in Ruby's shoes and thought about the stress she must have been under. In a journal entry by Clarita's mother, Clara Bartley, included in the statements below, she stated she believed Ruby had no idea what Ray was doing. But she stated Ruby had seen bank transactions showing monies given to the men in Ray's life and she "put a stop to it," causing Clara to think Ruby was catching on. If Ruby had found out, it would have been very distressing. We know she was pleading with Ray to not divorce her, and marital troubles can cause intense stress. That might or might not explain some of her negative behavior as described by Mary Claire in her statement.

I also want to add, according to Ray, Ruby's housekeeping and hygiene was a point of contention. Again, things are always magnified during times of duress. I imagine Ruby's home was much like many homes from that era. Crowded and cluttered. I remember visiting several of my great aunts' (Ruby's sisters) homes and observing rooms behind closed doors as being stacked to the ceiling with miscellaneous items. Even on my paternal side of the family my great grandma had an area in her Victorian home where I would "pilfer" through all the random items. I need not mention my grandma's home. It could be the era, or it could be a family trait. But no doubt about it, Ruby might have had the tendency to hoard things. That behavior doesn't diminish her value as a person though.

In Ray's statement, he mentions spending $4,000 on one person. I wondered how much that would be in today's time, so I looked it up. The value of $4,000 in 1963 is equal to $40,000 in 2024. The value of $100 in 1963 is equal to $1,000 in 2024. Ray stated he would give anywhere from $10-$100 to the men he talks about. Ray's salary was $6,500 a year. That puts these amounts in perspective.

These statements hold details that are valuable in piecing together the clues to unravel this mystery. Looking through the lens of an investigator, one would be watching for inconsistencies, hesitations, contradictions, or overly rehearsed responses, among other behaviors. An investigator would hear the minor details such as Ruby being "messy" but look at the big picture to piece this puzzle together.

Mary Claire Stapleton
◈◈

Supplement #4

I, Mary Claire Stapleton, give the following voluntary statement to W.A. Tudor, Arkansas State Police at the White County Courthouse in Searcy, AR on October 14th, 1963.

On Tuesday, October 8th, 1963, I had classes from 8:00 a.m. till 11:30 a.m. and I saw my mother at noon, had lunch at home with my mother and went back to class at 1:00 p.m. If I remember, I was at the library studying after lunch and before 1:00. I got out of classes at 2:50 p.m. and went straight to the library for more study. And I didn't leave the library until about 5:30. I ate supper at home with my mother and Clarita Bartley, my cousin. I went back to the campus at 6:30 and to the Missionary club meeting at 6:30 p.m. I went directly from the club meeting to the library, staying until about 10:00 p.m. Then I went straight home.

When I arrived at the house, Mother wasn't home, and I talked with Clarita, who was the only one present at the house, and Clarita told me that mother had gone to the washateria to wash clothes. I talked with Clarita about nothing in particular until 11:00 or 11:30. I began to worry that my mother wasn't home, and I asked Clarita if I should call the launderama, and Clarita thought that I should I try to find a phone number for the launderama, and we couldn't find a number. I waited until about midnight when I called the police and told them my mother had heart trouble, who I was, where I lived and that my mother had been gone 2 1/2 hours and that if the police had a man out in the area of the laundromat by Harrison's grocery would they please check on my mother. The police agreed to do that. A few minutes later the police called me and said that they had found my mother's car at the launderama but that she wasn't there.

I told the police that my mother could be out at Glen Dewey 's mother in laws, the Rhodes and that I would call out there. I called the Rhodes and learned that mother had been out there hours before but wasn't there now. I told Mrs. Rhodes that I was going to have the police come get me and we talked about telling Glen Dewey and we speculated that she may have been sick and taken to the hospital. I thought we would look for mother about an hour and if we didn't find Mother by then, I would tell Glen Dewey. The police took me out to the laundromat, and I saw my mother's car parked in front of the place, but she wasn't there. I thought then maybe Glen Dewey and Pat had come by and taken Mother to their house. Mr. Hunter drove me out to Glen Dewey's, and I knocked on the door. It took them a while to wake up, 5 minutes, and I told them what had happened. They couldn't imagine what happened. Mr. Hunter left me at Glen Dewey's house. Glen Dewey and Pat dressed, and we all took the children and left the house. We left James Earl at Mrs. Rhodes house and kept the baby with us. We stopped at the launderama and there was some policeman there. The police asked if we had a picture of Mother. We went home and got one, then took the picture down to the police station.

On this Tuesday, Mother got up early as usual, about 5:00 a.m. Mother had my breakfast ready, and I gulped down my breakfast about 7:30 a.m. and ran to classes. Clarita didn't have to get up early because of no early classes, and I ate alone. Mother ate early as usual. I don't remember that Mother was in the kitchen, but I do remember breakfast was on the table and beginning to get cold. I don't remember talking with my mother at all. At noon Mother, Clarita and I ate lunch at 12:30, and I remembered it was a good lunch and all three of us had a pleasant and happy conversation at the table.

At the supper meal, I was home about 5:30 and Mother was out puttering around. Mother came in and asked Clarita and me what we wanted for supper. It was getting pretty late. About 6:00 p.m. Clarita ate a sandwich and I told Mother I didn't care what I ate and I went into the bathroom to fix my hair. And when I came out about 6:15, Mother was standing there with nothing fixed for me to eat. I asked her why she didn't fix me something to eat and she told me she didn't know what I wanted to eat. I told her she could have walked down to the bathroom and asked me. I don't remember that she said anything. I thought at the time this was unusual. Because she normally fixed me anything she had handy when I told her that I didn't care what I ate. She also normally rushed around and fixed me something to eat when I was in a rush for classes or other activities. On this evening when I entered the room, she was simply standing and looking out the window. This is something that mother rarely or never did before. Mother is just like a fire engine going 90 to nothing all the time.

During the morning this Tuesday, mother went to Louise's beauty shop and had her hair fixed. Her hair was very pretty at noon, and I remember I complimented her about it. She would have her hair fixed, I estimate, on an average about once each six weeks. I had planned to fix it for her, but I had been so busy lately and she decided to let Louise fix it again. I have been very frank with Mother and have given her much constructive criticism about her housekeeping, meals, expenses and told her she had hurt my feelings about many things. Mother apologized and said she would try to do better, and she did. When she would show Clarita and me consideration, we would both thank her, and we would complement her on the improvements she had made. I've lived all my life in a home and house of disorganization, confusion, chaos, and lack of affection. Mother wants to do everything for me but wants my life to be just like she arranges it. She treats me now, just exactly like she did when I was a little child. I cannot live a normal life around my mother and the environment of my house. Last year I attended David Lipscomb College for the entire school year and did so just to see if I could lead a normal life among normal people. I enjoyed it very much.

My reason for returning to Harding this school year was due to finances and academic reasons. I can go to school for a lot less money here. I have never been given a weekly allowance and mother would give me money when she thought I needed it. After my father separated from my mother nine years ago, he sent us a part of his check, I think about half for the first couple of years and then he has sent less and less until he now sends me only money to buy some of my clothes. I enjoy visiting with my father and I feel a very deep love for my father and a very deep sympathy for him. I feel my mother has ruined my father, weakened his faith in God, and I wonder now why he is still sane. Misplaced values, in every sense, was the trouble between my mother and father. Everything that he was for, she was against. She had no value for his opinion and paid no attention to how he wanted the house run. My mother had no regard for her personal hygiene or appearance. She is extremely hypercritical, and I've pointed this out to her very frankly many times and she refused to admit or think about it. My mother is just opposite to everything my father represents. Mother knew we hated and despised her actions and thinking. I have had many violent arguments with her and sometimes I have a guilty complex because of the way I talked to her. But I do not respect my mother's actions because she does what everybody else preaches against. My mother has told me she wished I didn't hate her so and wished she was out of my way. I have tried to explain that I didn't hate her. My mother behaves like the devil has a hold of her and I think she is insane. If my mother behaved away from home the way she does at home, no one would speak to her. I have thought of leaving home, but I want to finish my Christian education before I leave. My mother could walk into the room and cause me to just get the jitters and fall apart, making me feel so inferior with her comments. At other times she could be sweet and pleasant. During this past summer, I kept feeling that mother and I were hating each other more and more. And I felt like it was a situation that was getting worse and worse. Mother didn't write me for over a month, and I wrote her a blunt letter, that I didn't mail, telling her pretty well the way I felt. After I got back from camp, things were different. The house being moved and all. Things got back to normal before long, and there was some friction between mother and me, but we haven't argued violently. I have tried to reason more with mother when she hurts me. Clarita stays out of our arguments and she accepts Mother for what she is and tries to ignore the unpleasantries. Glen Dewey is hot headed and feels toward Mother the same as I do. I respect Mother for the good that is in her, but I hate what she has done to my father, and I hate the actions she has done. If I knew my mother was alive and safe and would return, I would only stay here as long as my father was here. I just can't stand my mother. She has ruined my father, driven him from our home and made home a hell on earth. My father couldn't live with mother because she is so filthy and for the many reasons I have already talked about. In summary, Mother couldn't be normal, and I feel like she doesn't know what she is and she is the victim of the worst kind of self-delusion possible. Glen Dewey and I are very compatible, and we seldom disagree. I trust his judgment and thinking. I think he is just the best brother I could have, and I love him very much. I hope my mother isn't or hasn't suffered, and I hope she won't. If mother is dead, I hope she had time to make things right with God. If she should come back and has lost her mind, I want her to be comfortably cared for and not to worry about a thing. I don't want her to go through the things we are going through. If she comes back all right, I'll get along with what I can, take care of myself and my things and if my father is with me, I'll get along fine.

End Statement

Charlotte Rhodes

❖❖

Glen Dewey's 14-year-old sister-in-law

Supplement #2

On Tuesday, October 8th, 1963, I was at home outside the house, when Mrs. Stapleton drove her station wagon up to the front of the house. It was about 7:30 p.m. She said she had brought some bones for my dog, and I started to open her car door and she said just wait until we come back by. She had called out to the house earlier and made arrangements for me to go to Pat and Glen Dewey's house. I got into the station wagon with Mrs. Stapleton, and we drove to Glen Dewey's house. I didn't notice what was in the station wagon. Glen

Dewey, Pat, and the children were at home. We went into the house and stayed until about 9:00 p.m.

After we got in the house, we just talked a while. I don't remember a single thing that was said, but I do remember that Pat went outside to see about the washer, and she called to Glen Dewey and told him something was wrong with the washer. Glen Dewey went outside, and Mrs. Stapleton followed him. I stayed in the house and watched TV for a while, then went on outside where they were. The washer is in the utility room located at the end of the carport. Mrs. Stapleton was standing inside the utility room with Pat and Glen Dewey and I stood near the utility room near the open door. Glen Dewey saw that he couldn't fix the washing machine, and Mrs. Stapleton told Pat and Glen Dewey she would take their clothes to the washateria and wash them with her clothes because she had planned to wash her clothes that night. Glen Dewey put a large basket of clothes in the car and Pat put a smaller basket in.

I remember Mrs. Stapleton asked Glen Dewey if he had clothes to wear the next day, and he told her he needed a pair of Levi's. She told him she would bring the Levi's back and either put them on a drying rack out in the carport by the door that night so as to not disturb Glen Dewey or Pat, and she would see them the next morning. Mrs. Stapleton and I started driving home and she stopped on the shoulder of the road near the intersection of US767B and the old highway and asked me if I got the Wisk. I told her I didn't know, and she asked me to look in the back of the station wagon and see. I looked and told her I didn't see it and when she stopped, she looked too and couldn't find it. Then she said that she guessed Tide would do just as well. We drove to my house, and I started to get out. She told me to not forget the bones. I got the sack of bones out of the car and Mrs. Stapleton waited until I got into the garage and turned on the light before she drove off. She stayed in the car during this time.

I remember Miss Stapleton told Glen Dewey and Pat just before we left their house, that she would take Pat and the baby to the doctor the next day for their check up and she would take the oldest boy, James Earl, to get a pair of shoes while Pat and the baby were at the doctor's office. I haven't seen Miss Stapleton since she left me at my house at 9:05 p.m. on this Tuesday.
End Statement.

Clarita Dorothea Bartley

❖❖

Ruby's 20-year-old niece

Supplement #3

I, Clarita Bartley, give the following voluntary statement to Sergeant W.A. Tudor, Arkansas State Police at the White County Courthouse, Searcy, AR on October 14th, 1963.

I moved into the Stapleton House on September 9th, 1961, and I have lived there during the school term since. I am now a junior at Harding College.

Tuesday, October 8th, 1963, I woke at 7:30 a.m. and had breakfast alone. Breakfast was already prepared and on the table. I don't recall what I ate, and I don't recall seeing Mrs. Stapleton before I left, but I heard her say bye to me. I attended classes during the morning and returned to the Stapleton house for lunch. Mrs. Stapleton was standing at the sink, and I remarked that her hair was beautiful. She had been to the beauty shop earlier in the day. Mary Claire, Mrs. Stapleton, and I ate lunch together and had a pleasant conversation at lunch. We talked so long that I was late for my class at 1 o'clock p.m. I returned to the Stapleton house at 5:30, and I think Mary Claire walked home with Jerry Baker and me. Mrs. Stapleton was standing at the stove and Jerry came in with us. Jerry had a conversation with Mrs. Stapleton concerning a missionary, Brother Picarrds, and Mrs. Stapleton remarked that she knew this missionary very well. Jerry left in just a few minutes, and I walked outside with Jerry. I went back in and ate supper that Mrs. Stapleton had fixed. It was a sort of mixed vegetable stew. I know that Mary Claire ate with me, but I'm not sure that Mrs. Stapleton ate with us after supper. I left for the Bible building with Mary Claire and we got there shortly after 6:30 p.m. after the meeting, and Jerry and Ralph McCluggage talked with Mary Claire and me at their room for a while. We all walked out of the building together, and Mary Claire walked on to the library.

Within a few minutes, Jerry and I went on to the library for a while and Jerry and I took a walk. We left the library about 8 o'clock or 8:15 p.m. Jerry walked me home and it was 9:10 when we got to the Stapleton house. Jerry left and I walked to the back of the house, saw that the door was locked. I walked over to the hydrant and started cleaning off my shoes. At about 9:12, Mrs. Stapleton drove up and asked me what had happened. I told her and she got me a bucket to wash my shoes in and I put the sweater in the bucket and carried my shoes in my hand; went through the back door into the house. I waited for Mrs. Stapleton while she went to the side porch and got my books. Mrs. Stapleton told me she was going to do the laundry by Harrison's grocery to wash clothes. She told me she didn't want to wash the life out of her clothes and there was a 20-minute cycle at that laundry. Mrs. Stapleton was alone when she came home at this time.

I went upstairs and Mrs. Stapleton went into another room, I presume to get her clothes. Mrs. Stapleton left within a few minutes and told me she would be back as soon as she could. I haven't seen her since.

Mary Claire came home about 10:00 p.m. and we talked a long time until she went downstairs to study. I was sitting upstairs rolling my hair and Mary Claire said she was worried about her mother. About midnight she said she was real worried about her mother but couldn't find the phone number. She then called the police and asked them to look in on Mrs. Stapleton. The police called back and said Mrs. Stapleton's car was there, but she wasn't. Mary Claire asked the police to come for her and they did. I locked the doors and stayed home.

Later in the night, Glen Dewey and Mary Claire came to the house and wanted to get a picture of Mrs. Stapleton to give to the police. They made several phone calls while they were there and then left the house and took the picture to the police.

Glen Dewey came back and told me about the break-ins and I told him I would stay with the phone.

Mary Claire called later in the morning and told me she was out at the Rhodes. I told Mary Claire I was scared and worried and that I was thinking of calling Ralph and Jerry to stay with me. She said that she thought I should. I did, and they came to stay the rest of the night.

Both Aunt Ruby and Mary Claire have hot tempers, and she doesn't mean to make you feel inferior, but she continuously kept doing things for me that I had rather do for myself.

She and Mary Claire argued frequently year before last and then Mary Claire was away last year. After Mary Claire came back this year, things are much better and we had a devotional each evening, just the three of us, and I have remarked to Mary Claire that the three of us were much closer recently.

As far as the situation around the house, my main complaint was the meals; we ate horribly. But I love Aunt Ruby and generally I got along with her very well. Aunt Ruby just wouldn't let me fix my own meals, and her meals were just not up to par. She confided to me about how she felt, what she was worried about, etc.

Mrs. Stapleton was a messy housekeeper, was not clean herself, and I can understand why Mr. Stapleton might not want to live with her. I don't really know why they are separated, but I know she was not one to show affection and she neglected her family for everything else.

Last year, Aunt Ruby and I lived alone during the school year at Harding, while Mary Claire attended an out-of-town college and during this school year, Aunt Ruby confided in me occasionally, and I became very close to her and very fond of her.

I know Aunt Ruby kept a carbon copy of each letter, both personal and business, that she wrote and on one occasion, back last spring, I was nosy enough to read one of her letters to Uncle Ray. In this letter, she was begging Uncle Ray not to get a divorce and telling him she would sell the property to the college if he would not go through with his divorce plans and if he would stay away from Searcy while she accumulated the sale. In another part of this letter, she asked Uncle Ray to go to the F.B.I. with his problem of being harassed by his men friends who were asking him for money because these men "would stop at nothing" and that the matter would get worse and worse. Within a few weeks, Uncle Ray came to Searcy and was with Aunt Ruby when they sold this property to the college.

I have often heard Mary Claire use very abusive language toward her mother, and many times I have told Mary Claire she should be ashamed to talk to her mother in such a manner. Most of Mary Claire's trouble with her mother was just minor things which would irritate Mary Claire until she lost her temper and became violently angry.

Glen Dewey was closer to his mother than Mary Claire, but they often argued about small matters. Although Mary Claire may tell you she hates her mother, I believe she is just emotionally upset and is being influenced by her father when she makes these statements.

Before I came here to talk with you, Uncle Ray told me specifically to be very emphatic when you questioned me about certain things, including telling you that I did not think Aunt Ruby would ever be involved with another man. He also asked me to be sure and remember any names and persons that you asked me about.

Uncle Ray has talked to Mary Claire at great length and privately each evening that he has been here since Aunt Ruby's disappearance, and I think he is attempting to influence her against her mother by telling her many stories about why they are separated.

End Statement

Glen Dewey Stapleton

❖❖

Ray and Ruby's 25-year-old son

Glen Dewey furnished investigators with a brief history of himself and his family. I was interested by the background information regarding his upbringing. He gives key insight to the family dynamic, and it is interesting to hear his perspective on his family's relationships. Glen Dewey's perspective is somewhat different than his sister, Mary Claire's. I am hopeful this will provide history that is of interest to the remaining family of Ruby, if nothing else.

Supplement #5

I, Glen Dewey Stapleton give the following voluntary statement to Benson Robbins, Chief Deputy Sheriff, White County, and Sergeant W.A. Tudor, Arkansas State Police at the courthouse in Searcy, AR on October 17th, 1963.

I was born in Arab, AL, March 15th, 1938, while my parents,

Emmett Ray and Ruby Lowery Stapleton were teaching there or working there. My family moved to Searcy when I was just a baby, and we lived there until I completed the first grade of Harding Training School. My family then moved to Iowa City, IA, where mother and daddy both attended school for one semester. We then moved to Norman, OK and we were there the second semester of the year while my parents attended school and we remained at Norman, OK while I finished the third grade there. We came back to Searcy and moved into a house at 904 E Center St. where I lived with both my parents until my father left to teach at Northeast Louisiana State College in Monroe, LA. I graduated from Harding Academy in 1955 and I lacked part of a credit at that time. I attended Harding College for about 9 weeks to make this deficit.

I started in the spring of 1956 at the Beebe Junior College after working the summer as a driver for the county bookmobile and finished that semester. I broke my ankle and didn't finish out this first year of school. After recovering from this ankle injury, I went to work for Chub Smith Service Station in Searcy and for the Arkansas Appraisal Service. During the latter part of 1957, I began work for the Clary Corporation and worked there until the later part of 1959. I then went to work for Truman Baker and worked nine months for him before I had a knee operation in 1960. Right after my knee was operated on, I went to Commerce, Texas and attended summer school at East Texas State College.

My sister and I both went to summer school that summer and lived with my father in his house at 1321 Greenville Street. I attended classes in the morning and worked at the Ward Manufacturing Company in Greenville, TX, about 20 miles away during the afternoon and evening. I worked eight hours a day. My father was living alone except for my sister who had preceded me there a few days, and we all lived in the house together during the summer.

Once, while my mother, sister, and I were visiting my father at his house in Commerce, TX, during 1957 or 1958, we were introduced to a man named Grady Bankhead, who was in my father's house when we arrived for this visit. The man shook hands with me and left abruptly and went into another room. This man stayed clear of us, and I recall that he left the house once and returned before our visit was over. We stayed, this trip, about 24 hours. The only remark that I can remember my father making was that he felt sorry for "Old Bankhead" and that the man had very few friends.

In September on the 11th, I was married in Searcy to Pat Rhodes, and we moved to Commerce TX, where we moved into a duplex during September 1960. I intended to go to school and work at Ward's Manufacturing Company. I was still working at Ward's, and we were returning to Texas after a trip when we were involved in a wreck near Jacksonville. Due to the wreck and financial reasons, I decided not to go the first semester. I continued to live in Commerce, TX, and work at Ward's. During March 1961, Pat and I moved back to Searcy, and I went to work for Matthews Bronze Company, and I still work there.

Pat and I have two children. The oldest is James Earl, age 2 ½, and the youngest is Gary Lee and he is 9 weeks old. All I can say about my life at home with my parents is that mother helped me with my lessons when I needed help, tried to instill in my mind all the religion that she could, tried to teach me the right thing and see that I did it, fixed ample and good meals, showed affection towards me and the rest of the family, and even though I am married and have a family, my family and I normally ate Sunday dinners with my mother until she disappeared. Let me say that my mother had a full-time job with her teaching, and she had to let her house go to keep up with her work. She had little regard for her personal appearance, and she was very cautious with her spending. I don't know the reasons for my father leaving home, it was never discussed with me, but after he left, my mother tried to be both a mother and father to me and I love her very much. We have had a few family disagreements, but nothing violent. Mary Claire and mother argued often, Mary Claire being emotional and actually being upset more because of Mother's poor housekeeping and the like. Another thing, my grandfather Lowery was a fine man and I loved him very much, but he was the type of man that thought he could do everything better than anyone else. Some of this thinking must have been inherited by my mother. This attitude of mother often caused Mary Claire to be upset. Let me also say that Mary Claire always seemed to be closer to my father than my mother, even while he was away. It was the other way with me. I enjoyed my father every day that he was home, but after he left, I have had very little contact with him and thus have been drawn closer to my mother.

Last year, my parents sold a portion of an acreage they owned south of Searcy to Erving's hatchery. I don't know what the sale price was or why it was sold, but I do know that Mother had talked with people representing White County Memorial Gardens sometime before the actual sale.

Last spring, I, my family and myself, was living in a house at 903 E. Center Street owned by my parents and located next door to their house. We paid mother rent on this, and I was in the process of cleaning the place up. My parents had planned for some time even before I was married, that they would give me this place that I was living in. This past spring, my parents gave us this house. Later in the spring, Dr. Benson called and asked when he could see me and talk to me about selling this place. Mother made arrangements for me to meet him at Mother's house. I ultimately sold the place to the college for $11,000. A short time later, my parents made a deal with the college and sold the property that was adjoining my place. This sale was also to the college, and I don't know what the price was or what prompted my parents to sell this property.

Pat and I looked around searching for a place to build a house and any property that we could afford was not suitable. Mother remarked to me that I should build on a part of the acreage she and daddy owned that is across from the Searcy Airport. I didn't want to build there because it is known as Tornado Alley, but Pat and I decided to buy three acres of this property from my parents and pay them $1,000 for it. Later mother said that she and daddy, or we've, decided to give Pat and me the acreage. I offered to pay her for this property, and she wouldn't accept. She told me that she would deed this property to me, and I am checking now to see if this has been done. I have hired a contractor that has built me a home on this acreage described above.

Last Tuesday, October 8th, 1963, I worked at Matthews Bronze Company in Searcy until 3:30 p.m. and then drove home. About 7:00 p.m. I went to the airport; there is a phone there, and I called John Osborne at Searcy, and he works with me out at Matthews. I talked to him about working on my washer and asked him if he would come out. I explained to him that the washer wasn't working properly, and Pat had put a load in the washer.

Soon after I called Osborne, he came out to the house, and he told me that he believed it was something that I could fix. He told me that there was a restriction in the hose or pump and that it was stopped up. Osborne was there about 15 or 25 minutes, and he left.

Before 8:00 p.m. my mother drove up to my house in her station wagon and Charlotte Rhodes was with her. Mother and Charlotte visited with us until about 9:00 p.m. and at that time I hadn't been able to repair the washer. Mother volunteered to take our clothes to the laundromat and do them while she did her wash that night. I put the clothes in Mother's car and she and Charlotte left about 9:00 p.m.

Pat and I went to bed about 10:30 p.m. and we heard or saw nothing unusual after Mother left us. After Mother left, we simply closed up the house, watched television a little while, and I shaved and bathed, then we went to bed.

Mary Claire and a policeman came to my house about 1:00 a.m. and told me that mother was missing.

I have read the above 1 1/2 page and find it correct to the best of my knowledge.

End Statement

E.R. Stapleton

❖❖

Supplement #6 October 6th, 14[th,] and 17th

E.R. Stapleton, husband of the victim, was interviewed in Searcy, AR at 11:00 a.m. October 10th, 1963, and related that he was then engaged in teaching at Superior State College, Superior, WI where he had been so employed since the first week of September 1963. Stapleton continued by stating that he had last seen his wife during the last few days of August 1963, at the time of his departure from Searcy enroute to Superior WI and that he had communicated with her, both by phone and letter, on two or three occasions after his departure.

When questioned about his opinion regarding the victim's disappearance, he replied that his only thought was abduction by transients, possibly Mexicans who traveled the area between Illinois and Texas. He elaborated on this theory by stating that his wife was very dark complexioned and had the appearance of being of Spanish descent. He remarked that his wife had led a "golden life," was very dedicated to the church and school and had constantly worked toward a goal in her life. He denied when questioned that he was separated from his wife due to marital troubles and was quick to express that he loved his wife very much, kept in very close contact with her and the family, and his only reason for working away from home was due to a disagreement with policy at Harding College. Stapleton remarked that he was trying his best to bear up under his wife's disappearance and make the best of the situation because of his daughter's grief.

Stapleton states that he wants to assure investigators of his complete cooperation in this matter, and at this point in the conversation, he began to sob and cry. After the tears were dried away, he made the remark that his wife was loved by everyone, and his only complaint, ever, was that she had lost her sense of values and appeared more dedicated to the church and school than to her home.

Within an hour after the initial contact with E.R. Stapleton, investigators received a telephone call at the Sheriff's Office in Searcy, relating that the man who had kidnapped the victim was now on the telephone attempting to extort money from E.R. Stapleton. Investigators traveled to the scene, contacted telephone officials, and traced the call to a phone booth in Lubbock, TX. Officers in that city were notified and within minutes had arrested Gray F. Chandler while he was still engaged in conversation with E.R. Stapleton. Chandler's associate Karl Karash was standing by the telephone and both were lodged in jail at Lubbock, TX. The information regarding this call was furnished to the F.B.I., who interviewed both subjects in Lubbock and E.R. Stapleton at Searcy before charging Karash and Chandler with the federal violation of "Fraud by Wire."

During the interview of E.R. Stapleton by Ed Brown, Special Agent, F.B.I., Little Rock, AR and Investigators, Stapleton remarked that he had met both Chandler and Karash while he was instructing at Appalachian State Teachers College at Boone, NC, specifically met Chandler, at Boone, NC, and Karash at Christiansburg, VA, both during the spring of 1963. He stated that he had simply picked them up while they were hitchhiking, befriended them, let them stay at his place a few days, and furnished them small amounts of money. He admits that both Karash and Chandler have called him collect a "few times," asking him for money, and that he has sent the money, no more than $10 on each of these occasions.

He related that Chandler had called him from Morrilton, AR during August 1963 and that he had brought him to Beebe, placed him in a motel, then transported him to Little Rock the following day, where they had dinner with the victims. Stapleton signed a statement made to the F.B.I. concerning the above information and relating that Chandler had attempted to obtain money from him by remarking that if Stapleton did not send him money, Chandler had another alternative.

A few days later, E.R. Stapleton was again interviewed at the courthouse in Searcy and questioned about the sale of property during 1962 and 1963, owned jointly by Stapleton and the victim. Stapleton remarked that on or about May 1962, the victim sold an acreage located South of Searcy across US 67 to a hatchery at Searcy and stated that he did not know the amount of money obtained for this property. He stated that his wife had sold in about June 1963 some property adjacent to their dwelling to Harding College and again stated that he knew nothing about how much money was obtained from the sale of this property. He remarks that his wife handled all the money matters and that he willfully accepted the money offered him as his part. Stapleton then remarked that his salary at Superior State College is $7,700 per year, and he was paid $6,500 for his years teaching at Boone, NC.

When questioned about finances Stapleton stated that he has about $300 in a checking account at the Northwestern Bank in Boone, North Carolina, and a small checking account at the First National Bank, Superior, Wisconsin. He states that he made a deposit at the First National Bank, Wolfe City, Texas, after receiving almost $8,000 from the sale of the property to Harding College, and that this entire amount was now held by that bank on a checking account. He related that he had not spent this money and had placed it in that bank until he made up his mind what he wanted to do with these funds. He states that he had no knowledge of the current bank account maintained by the victim but did recall that they had a joint banking account at the Security Bank in Searcy Arkansas when he last wrote a check on that account during the past fall.

Investigators then questioned Doctor Stapleton about his associations with homosexuals, and he told a long and descriptive story about his past experience and admitted performing actual homosexual acts on numerous occasions with many individuals, most of whom he did not know the names, and some whose names were furnished and are listed as follows:

Continued police notes marked as Supplement #7
Listed as facts.

Roy Whitfield, now working as a missionary and who at the time of these homosexual acts during the early 1930s, was a student at Harding College, Searcy, AR.

Clarence Heflinger, who at the time of these homosexual acts during 1951 was a professor at Harding College.

Douglas Martin, who lived in an apartment with Stapleton while Stapleton taught at Northeast Louisiana State College, Monroe, LA. And who attempted to blackmail Stapleton during the Commission of these homosexual acts.

Grady Bankhead, who lived with Stapleton while he taught at East Texas State College. Commerce, Texas.

Douglas Daugherty, who lived with Stapleton while he taught at East Texas State College, Commerce, Texas.

Billy Joe Rust, who lived with Stapleton while he taught at East Texas State College, Commerce, Texas.

Karl Karash, who is now in custody of the US Marshall at Lubbock, TX and he lived with Stapleton while he taught at Boone, NC.

Gray F Chandler, who is now in custody of the US Marshall at

Lubbock, TX and who lived with Stapleton while he taught at Boone, NC.

Jack Irvine, who lived with Stapleton while he taught at Boone, North Carolina.

Dalon Dean Barnes lived with Stapleton when he taught at Boone, NC.

The name James Douglas Daugherty was not furnished voluntarily by Stapleton in this questioning and was obtained by investigators from a record of long-distance calls made by Stapleton during the past few months. Stapleton had completed his list of homosexuals whose names were known to him and whom he had enjoyed "affairs in my house" and had been in the process of trying to rack his brain to tell of any others that he might recall their names. Stapleton was given an opportunity to think for several minutes and then he made the statement that there were many others but that he could recall no other names and certainly had no long-prolonged affairs with any persons not already mentioned to us.

Stapleton was then asked if he knew Douglas Daugherty. He showed great surprise, raised up abruptly in his chair, and exclaimed, my word, man, where did you get that name? Investigators did not answer his question and then asked him what his relation with Douglas Daugherty had been.

Stapleton regained his composure and stated that he had met Douglas Daugherty after Daugherty had been pointed out to him by another homosexual, who Stapleton refused to name, and had approached Daugherty about performing homosexual acts with Stapleton. Daugherty consented and lived in Stapleton's house occasionally and rented rooms and at some time performed these acts in an automobile. Stapleton travelled with Douglas Daugherty to his home near Canton, TX and met his parents. On that occasion he learned that Douglas Daugherty was 15 years old. He told of visiting and seeing Daugherty intermittently for several years and giving him small sums of money. Buying his meals and paying for his bowling during this time.

Stapleton then began to tell officers a long and detailed story of why he was practicing homosexual acts, and blamed the matter entirely on his wife, made remarks that she had driven him to his present state of mind, and that he hated his wife, and hoped that he never saw her again. He stated that his children, both Mary Claire and Glen Dewey, had made remarks to him indicating that they hoped they never saw their mother again.

On October 17th, 1963, a written statement was obtained from E.R. Stapleton, of which a copy is attached to this report as Supplement #8.

In this statement Stapleton reviews information previously furnished to investigators in other statements and elaborates in more detail on his contacts with James Douglas Daugherty, and his common law wife Louise Marcum. He admits that Daugherty had written him a letter as recently as early October 1963, asking for another thousand dollars. The following is the last paragraph of his statement:

"Normally, I spend no more than $10 or $15 on a man to have him love me, and I have spent $85 on one occasion to have a man love me for one night. But there is no comparison between this type of spending and the money that I have spent on Douglas Daugherty. I estimate that I have spent at least $4,000 on Douglas Daugherty already. Mainly for his love and affection. He pleases me and I love him very much. If I love my wife like I do Douglas Daugherty, I wouldn't let her out of my sight. But I don't want any sex at all with him, and my sex experiences with Douglas have been very, very few. I only want from Douglas Daugherty is for him to just love the hell out of me. I wanted to give him this education and spend money on his education. Just so that he would live with me and love me."

After furnishing investigators with this written statement, Stapleton was questioned about any opinion he now might have about motive for his wife's disappearance. He stated that he had appeared to many, including Douglas Daugherty and Louise Marcum, as a free spender and had made remarks indicating that he and the victim owned jointly, real estate and other properties in the Searcy area. He relates that this conversation might tend to cause unscrupulous individuals to destroy the victim in an effort to get at the money and property, which would then be Stapleton's sole property. He remarked that most of these individuals knew that if he had property and wanted "loving" bad enough that they would have everything he owned. He further stated that he had concealed a fear for the victim's safety for the past year due to the facts mentioned above but had not discussed his thinking with her.

Investigators then proceeded to question Stapleton about numerous large checks that he had written on their joint account at Security Bank at Searcy while he was living at Boone, NC and Stapleton refused to discuss these checks and furnished his reason as his having been involved in an illegal action and he would not incriminate himself or his accomplice. Stapleton then admitted having spent most of the money deposited in the Wolfe City Bank and that he had written several large checks on this account to Daugherty.

Records at the Western Union office were examined by Lloyd Henry, prosecuting Attorney and Sergeant W.A. Tudor, and it was learned that E.R. Stapleton wired $50.00 to Gray F Chandler at the Western Union office in Los Angeles, CA on July 9th, 1963.

On July 13th, 1963, he wired $100 to the same man at the same place.

On July 22nd, 1963, Stapleton wired $50.00 to Gray F. Chandler at the Western Union office at Little Rock, AR.

This information is enclosed as Supplement #10 to this file.

The victims checking account at Security Bank. Searcy, AR, beginning September 12, 1962, and continuing through the day of her disappearance, was examined and information learned is enclosed with this report as Supplement #11.

Supplement #8 OCTOBER 17
E.R. STAPLETON

"I, Doctor E.R. Stapleton give the following voluntary statement to Benson Robbins, Deputy Sheriff, White County, and Sergeant W.A. Tudor, Arkansas State Police at the White County Courthouse in Searcy on October 17th, 1963."

"I was born at Hunt County, Texas, near Greenville on February 5th, 1905. My parents were farmers, and I grew up and finished high school at Wolfe City, TX in 1926. In the following summer I attended Tyler, TX Commercial College. In the next two years, I was a secretary to the Superintendent of the L&A Railway company, Minden, LA. During the fall of 1926, I came to Harding College at

Morrilton, AR as a freshman student and attended there continuously until I received a bachelor's degree in 1932. They retained me in the college division as a professor and I taught at Morrilton until they moved the school to Searcy. I continued to teach at Searcy until I was married in June 1935. Mrs. Stapleton and I moved to Baileyton, Alabama, where I was Secretary Treasurer of the Empire Nursery and Orchards Company for two years. In the school year of 1938 to 1939, I was Superintendent of schools at Aplin, Arkansas and Mrs. Stapleton was my principal teacher. In 1940 to 1941 school term Mrs. Stapleton and I moved back to Searcy and began teaching at Harding College where I taught until 1953. I resigned that year and Mrs. Stapleton continued to teach until her disappearance October 8th, 1963."

"After resigning at Harding College due to differences between myself and Doctor Benson, the President of Harding, about economic viewpoints and because of my desire and need to get away from Mrs. Stapleton, there was two years that I tried to farm and raise cattle on the Stags place and try to keep house for Mrs. Stapleton while she worked."

"From the very beginning of my marriage to Mrs. Stapleton, I was aware that she had no regard for her personal hygiene or appearance, and she constantly embarrassed me and the children. She wouldn't bathe with any regularity, and she would wear her underclothing until it actually fell apart from filth. During the first week of our marriage, I actually gagged while trying to have sex acts with my wife because of her terrible body odor, and things never got better. Mrs. Stapleton was as sexless as any woman could be and I deplored having anything to do with her sexually. She would wear clothing to teach and to church that was so filthy and dirty that it shouldn't even be worn at home. She kept her house just like she kept her person. The place was continuously a filth, piled up and chaotic. It embarrassed me always and the doors leading from the living room into the rest of the house were always kept closed and no visitor was ever allowed past the living room. This condition that I have described became more and more deplorable. My sex life with Mrs. Stapleton became unbearable and actually has caused me to have no desire for the female sex. This was brought on by time and time again my having discontinued our sex act because I had lost my composure due to her unbearable body odor and filthy condition. I talked with Mrs. Stapleton about this and begged her to bathe and clean herself up, but she paid no attention to me and wouldn't even make an excuse. She just thought that she was clean enough for anybody. Let me say that there were two things that she was immaculate about. This was her cooking and her cleaning and caring for the children.

"I have had homosexual tendencies from infancy due to this lack of love and affection, and this fact, coupled with my sexless life with Mrs. Stapleton, caused me to experiment with homosexuality while I was at Harding College. This experiment was with Roy Whitfield. He was a student at Harding College. Whitfield was not a homosexual, and both of us wanted affection, so we spent the night together three or four times. It was just a petting party, loving and kissing, and we would jack each other off."

"Several years after Whitfield left, I had an affair with Clarence Hefflinger, the professor of music department at Harding College. That affair was just numerous petting parties, the same as I had with Whitfield."

"After leaving Harding in 1953, I picked up a hitchhiker in Searcy. I don't know who he was, and he wasn't local. This man and I had a petting party on a side road and we both performed homosexual acts on each other. This was my first experience at an actual homosexual act. I didn't pay this man any money and it was just a mutual enjoyment for both of us. I was involved in a very few of such acts while I was in the Searcy area."

"In the fall of 1955, I took a teaching job with Northeast Louisiana State College at Monroe, LA. During my teaching career there, continuing through the spring of 1957, I engaged in several homosexual acts and recall having met Grady Bankhead, who I picked up as a hitchhiker near Monroe, on a very cold night. I took him home with me to spend the night and we performed this homosexual act at my house during the night. I gave him $5 and let him out on the highway next morning."

"Another man, Douglas Martin, was also a friend of mine in Monroe, LA. I picked him up on the highway west of Monroe, LA and took him home with me. This man was not an actual homosexual, but he would perform as one for me. This was how our sex act was performed. This man lived with me three to five weeks and was involved in numerous sex acts with me during that time.

The act was Martin performing for me a great majority of the time.

"Douglas Martin spent three to five weeks with me in my house near Monroe. He tried to blackmail me when I wouldn't buy him a comfortable automobile that he saw and wanted. Martin told me that if I didn't buy the car for him that he would tell the school that I had been sucking his dick instead of his sucking mine. I told him to go ahead and tell them, and he did. There was an investigation, and I became disgusted with the situation and resigned. After my resignation, I learned that Martin had ruined two other men the same way. Martin was about 22 years old and is from Vilonia, AR. His stepfather is named Foshee. The only money I gave Martin was a little spending money. I spent the summer in travel throughout the Central States, and during the fall of 1957 I took a job of teaching at East Texas State Teachers College in Commerce, TX and moved into a house at 1321 Greenville St. During the first two years I lived there, it was just catch as catch can. I had several homosexual acts with various individuals, but they for the most part didn't know my name and I don't know theirs. After I had lived there about two years Grady Bankhead, the man I had met and spent the night with, in Monroe, LA, while teaching there, called me collect from Morrilton, Arkansas, and asked if he could visit me. I had been in correspondence with Grady on several occasions since he visited me in Monroe. Bankhead did come to my house in Commerce and lived there with me and registered at the college in his brother's name under the GI Bill. He stayed with me at my house during the semester and we had several homosexual acts together. The F.B.I. was after Bankhead because of him registering in the name of his brother so he left me. I took him to Dallas, TX and put him out on South Erver St. about Christmas 1959 or 60. I had a letter or two from Bankhead shortly after I took him to Dallas, but I never did answer them."

"While Bankhead was living with me, he wanted us to move to the southwest and wanted me to will my property to him. I know that this man has a criminal record. I have heard him mention a penitentiary. Bankhead's mother is named McCardoll and she lives at Springhill, Alabama, and he told me that he once worked for the police department in Marshall, Texas. I bought Bankhead liquor and gave him very small amounts of money."

"During the fall of 1957 I picked up James Douglas Daugherty in the edge of Dallas, Texas, on Grand Avenue, after he was pointed out to me by another man who had been with him earlier and had stated that Douglas Daugherty was good company or something to that effect. I took Daugherty back to my house in Commerce, Texas, where he spent the night with me. At that time, he was 13 or 15 years old, 5'3, and weighed 210 pounds. Daugherty and I performed these petting parties with no sex involved, and Daugherty lived at Canton, Texas while I lived at Commerce. We spent nights at motels and at my house and I visited his home and met his folks and all. Those acts persisted until I left that college and took a coaching job at Frederick College, Portsmouth, Michigan, the fall of 1961."

"While at Frederick College I had no petting parties at all and I was very lonesome for Douglas Daugherty, so I drove to Dallas, Texas, and called his folk's home. They wouldn't tell me where he was, so I drove to Canton, Texas and asked his father. His father told me that he had got a girl pregnant and was married, then had run away from his wife. He told me that I would hear from Douglas soon. I drove on back to Frederick College and completed the year. I think I heard from Douglas by letter while I was at Frederick College, but I didn't see him."

"During the last week that I was at Frederick College, I picked up Jack Ervine on highway 17 near Portsmouth and the first time I was with him we had a party on a side road. He was not in Uniform, but he claimed that he was a sailor. Three or four weeks later I picked him up on the highway again and took him to my home to spend the night. He just stayed with me overnight and is the type of man who will do anything sexually for money or liquor. I would buy his beer and would give five or ten dollars along. I was with him only twice before school was out. I moved into Portsmouth the next week and Ervine came to my home frequently during the summer for more of those sex parties. Jack had told me that he had been in the Parine hospital at Portsmouth."

"While I was teaching at East Texas State College, I picked up Billy Joe Rust, near Big Town Shopping Center in Dallas, Texas and he had been dismissed from Huntsville Penitentiary that morning. His people live at Greenville, Texas. Rust was drinking heavily when I picked him up and I took him home with me. He stayed with me for three or four days. He ran out of liquor, and I was out of money, so he left and went home. I had infrequent petting parties with him since then and the last was a year ago this last Christmas. He and I spent the night together a year ago in Greenville, Texas. I think that Rust is a very dangerous person. He has always been satisfied with a pint of whiskey and had never demanded money from me. He will do anything for the other fellow for liquor or a little bit of money."

"During the summer I quit teaching at Frederick College, I traveled to Wolfe City, Texas, to visit my mother and then learned that Douglas Daugherty was back living with his wife and that they moved to Rockwall, Texas. I went to Rockwall and visited Douglas home with him and his wife and their baby girl. While I was there Douglas caught his wife out of earshot and asked if I would like to go out and park. I told him yes and we left in my car and parked near the lake for three or four hours and had a petting party with no sex involved. After this I went to Boone, North Carolina, and started teaching at Appalachian State college. During Christmas last year, I was in Bristol, Virginia, and picked up Albert Patrick on the street and learned that he was staying at the Haven of Rest Mission, and I took him to my home at Boone, NC. He stayed with me a week before Christmas, through the Holidays, and for a week or ten days after Christmas. Patrick and I had several sex parties while he stayed with me. I gave him small amounts of money and at one time he told me that he had been in prison during a riot, and I think the prison was Michigan State prison. Up in the spring, Patrick came by to visit with me again, ate a meal with me and we had no sex party. I didn't give him any money and a short time later I received a scorching letter from him, and by that time he knew my superior at the college, telling me to send him ten dollars or he would expose me to Doctor Yoder and the Dean of the College. I sent him 25 dollars and told him to expose me in any way that he wanted to and that I considered this nothing more of a threat. I also told him that he was just as guilty as me and I gave him the dictionary definition of blackmail. I told him not to let me hear of him anymore. I have heard from him only one other time, I don't know whether it was before or after the threat, but that time he wanted me to send him two dollars to the jail in Bristol for use to buy tobacco."

"During the spring this year I picked up Karl Karash in Christiansburg, Virginia and took him to my house in Boone, N.C. He claimed to be on his way to work as an orderly at a bit hospital in Ashley, N.C. He stayed with me two or three days and we had petting parties while he was there. This man was without a home and just travels from place to place. I took him to the bus station and bought him a ticket to Asheville, N.C. and I may have given him three or five dollars while he was there. The next contact I had with this man was when he called me from Knoxville, Tennessee, and wanted me to send him $10.00 and I told him I would send it as a matter of a loan, and I did just that. This call was to me here at Searcy Eastern time. The next time I saw Karash was when I had a flat, several weeks later, in Boone, N.C. and was at a filling station having this flat repaired.

"On this occasion, Karash showed up at the filling station with a man named Gray F. Chandler and I remember distinctly that this was on Sunday afternoon. Both Karash and Chandler went to my home and spent a week. I took them to Roanoke the following Saturday. When I took them away, I think I gave them $10.00 each. The next morning, I called Gray Chandler's Aunt in Asheville, N.C. and told her of Gray's visit the past week. This call was made because I wanted to find out more about Gray Chandler. I then called Gray at the hotel in Roanoke where I left Gray and Karash and told Gray about calling his aunt and that I felt better about it."

"The next contact I had with Gray Chandler was when he called me collect from Morrilton while I was in Searcy. This was early this past summer. He called and told me that he had been trying to hitch hike out of Morrilton for about three hours and he wanted me to send him some money to get to Little Rock where he could get a job and get out of this hot sun. I told him that I couldn't wire him money this late and that I planned to go to Little Rock on business the next day. I agreed to come to Morrilton and pick him up that day, take him to Beebe, put him in a motel and take him to Little Rock the next day. After I cleaned up, I drove to Morrilton and picked up Gray Chandler and drove to Beebe after we stopped in Conway and had a good meal. He registered at Deesa's Hotel, and he went to his room. I came on back home. The next morning, I went to Deesa's Hotel and had a petting party there with him. I then drove Gray Chandler to Little Rock and put him in the Capitol Hotel and paid for his room for a week. I then returned to Searcy after telling Gray that Mrs. Stapleton and I would be in Little Rock the next day and to meet in front of hotel at 7 p.m."

"The next night Mrs. Stapleton and I did go to Little Rock and went into the lobby of the Capitol Hotel where we contacted Gray Chandler. He went shopping with us and ate at Frank's Cafeteria. Mrs. Stapleton left Chandler in Little Rock after telling him that we would see him the next day. I had bought a foreign car from Earl D. Baker in Searcy, and I was going to bring this car to Little Rock for servicing and repair. Mrs. Stapleton and I drove back to Searcy and that night Mrs. Stapleton mentioned she would bake Gray a pie if I would pick out the pecans. I picked them out and she baked the pie. The next day I went to Little Rock and Chandler had already left as far as I could determine. I don't know where Chandler was before he showed up in Morrilton and called me. I gave Chandler some money, maybe $10 while in Little Rock. During this week that Chandler was in Little Rock, I made a trip to Pensacola, Florida for an interview and he went with me. This foreign car I talked about from Earl B. Baker in Searcy was bought for my daughter Mary Claire."

"The next contact I had with Gray F. Chandler was when he called me from Lubbock, Texas, October 10th, 1963, posing as Frank Stevens and calling me collect in an attempt to get me to send him some money."

"Since Christmas this past year, I called Douglas Daugherty's family and learned that he was now living in California and that I would hear from him. He wrote me at Boone, North Carolina and gave me his address and telephone number. There were several telephone calls and telegrams, and the arrangement was that he would come to Boone, N.C. and he did, arriving there about the middle of the spring and after Chandler and Karash were there. He stayed with me about three weeks, after driving from California in his automobile."

"I sent him $200-$300 dollars for this trip. Douglas Daugherty then called this woman that he had been living with out there and he left my place to go back out there. We wrote back and forth after that, and Daugherty wanted me to come to California."

"After my teaching was over in Boone, N.C. I returned to Searcy and picked up Mary Claire. I drove her to Las Vegas, N.M. and returned to Searcy by way of my mother's. I stayed in Searcy two or three weeks and then went on to Dallas then on to Los Angeles, California, on San Marino Ave. I visited with Douglas and the woman he is living with, Louise Marcum, and got an apartment on the next floor from theirs and lived there less than a week. When we went out for meals, I always picked up the tab and while I was visiting with them, I told Douglas, in the presence of Louise, that Mrs. Stapleton and I didn't have much money but that I had a few thousand dollars to put in on Douglas's education if he would only take advantage of it. Both seemed grateful and wanted to stay there but Douglas was still married to the woman in Texas and couldn't marry Louise. Douglas and Louise then decided to go to Texas so that Douglas could get his divorce and marry Louise. All of us left California together, in two automobiles, and Louise abandoned her children in California. We drove to El Paso, Texas and got a suite of rooms at a hotel. Louise, Douglas, and I went shopping and they bought a few clothes, I bought them a set of luggage. We drove to Dallas, and they went to his parents' home in Canton, Texas."

"My next contact with Douglas Daugherty was after Mrs. Stapleton and I had gone from Mary Claire and had returned to my mother's. I just telephoned from my mother's and told him of my situation and that I couldn't see him. My next contact with Daugherty was when I took Glen Dewey and Pat to visit my sister in Dallas during this past summer. While at my sister's house, I called Douglas and told him that I would enjoy having dinner with him and Louise, and we all had dinner together at the cafeteria. I met them at Terrel, Texas and drove them to Dallas where we ate. I took them back to Terrell and while we were at the bowling alley there, Louise and Douglas told me some sort of sob story there, and I wrote him a check for $300 to $500. I drove on back to Dallas and then on to Searcy.

"The next time I saw Douglas Daugherty was just before I went to Superior, WI to teach at Superior State College. I drove to Texarkana and Douglas and Louise drove from Dallas to meet me there. Doug had no phone and asked me to visit with him and Louise there, apparently for no particular purpose. They were my guests at Bryce's cafeteria. Then we went out to the airport. Douglas told me a story about being picked up by the law and that it was going to cost him 100 or so dollars. He showed me his ticket and I wrote him another check. It must have been $200 or $300. I then drove back to Searcy after telling Douglas and Louise that when and if I thought the time was right and Douglas knew what I meant, I still had this few $1,000 to spend on his education."

"That is the latest time that I have seen Douglas or Louise personally. I corresponded with Douglas while I was in Superior, both by letter and telegram. He wrote to tell me that Louise was leaving him and that he had to take Louise to California to pick up her children and take her and the children to West Virginia to her parents' house. He then asked me to send him $1,000 to buy tires and pay the expense of his trip. I wired him and told him that I wouldn't send him the money and told him to call me collect. He did call me collect and he told me that Louise had already gone, and I asked what he would do if she returned. He told me that he wouldn't have a damn thing to do with her, I told him that I was ready to go on with his education if and when I could believe that this was true. I asked him to write me a good letter."

"Douglas did write me a short letter after Glen Dewey called me and told me that Mrs. Stapleton had disappeared, I sent Douglas a telegraph asking him to call me at Searcy collect. I flew to Memphis and then traveled to Searcy. Douglas called me collect on the morning of the ninth saying that Louise had wired him that she was coming back. I asked him what he was going to do. He then said that he didn't know anything to do but accept her. I told him, that being the case, just forget about me entirely and that I was through with the whole thing, not to ask me for any money, not to contact me in any way and that my plans for his education was all off. I also told him that Mrs. Stapleton had disappeared. Douglas disappointed me in not evidencing more alarm or concern. He told me that he was sorry and told me that I knew that we could have petting parties anytime and that Louise didn't object. I know this because Douglas had told Louise and I had talked freely in front of Louise about my wanting to be loved by another man. Louise had stated that I could have "it" anytime that I wanted it, and I informed both Douglas and Louise that it wasn't "it" that I was interested in but only wanted a man's love and affection."

"Douglas begged me to allow him and Louise to come to Superior and said that he would put her to work, and, with my help, he could finish his high school work and get his college education. I told him, "No Doug, it's all off." He told me that he was sorry, and I told him that as long as he was involved with Louise, I didn't want any contact with him. That phone conversation is the last contact that I have had with Douglas Daugherty."

"All in all I recall furnishing Douglas Daugherty with the following money. I paid a thousand dollars on his new automobile while he was in Boone, N.C. last spring. Then during this last summer I wrote him checks for two or three hundred dollars, or possibly more or less, on two or three occasions, this past summer. In addition to these checks, I have appeared to be a free spender in the presence of Douglas and Louise. I do know that Douglas told me that his brother, Danny, was out of the navy, married, and had brought his wife to Canton, Texas. He had finally got a job then Louise told me at Texarkana that Danny's wife had left him."

"Normally I spend no more than 10 or 15 dollars on a man to have him love me, and I have spent $85 on one occasion to have a man love me for one night but there is no comparison between this type of spending and the money that I have spent on Douglas Daugherty. I estimate that I have spent at least $4,000 on Douglas Daugherty already, mainly for his love and affection. He pleases me and I love him very much. If I loved my wife like I do Douglas Daugherty, I wouldn't let her out of my sight, but I don't want any sex with him and my sex experiences with Douglas have been very very few. I only want from Douglas Daugherty is for him to just love the hell out of me. I wanted to give him this education, and spend money on his education, just so that he would live with me and love me."

I have read the above four- and one-half pages and to the best of my knowledge it is correct.

E.R. Stapleton

End Statement

Brief Summary of Ray's Employment

Supplement #52
Verification of past employment, E.R. Stapleton, and brief summary of work experience at these colleges.

F.B.I. agents at Superior, WI have verified that E.R. Stapleton has been employed on the teaching staff at Superior State College,

Superior, WI as Assistant Professor of Economics since the start of school term in September 1963 and has taught there continuously until October 9th, 1963. Ray resigned from his teaching position in Wisconsin shortly after Ruby's disappearance.

On that date the Colleges Administrative Assistance Eugene Olson transported Stapleton from Superior, WI to Duluth, MN where Stapleton caught a North Central Airlines flight at 1:00 p.m.

While in Superior, Stapleton resided at 1011 N. 18th St. Apt 3. Questioning of Stapleton's neighbors and persons residing in the apartment house failed to reveal information pertinent to this case. Questioning of his associates and the college failed to reveal knowledge indicating that they were aware of his homosexual tendencies.

F.B.I. agents in Boone, NC have verified that E.R. Stapleton was employed on the teaching staff at Appalachian State Teachers College, Boone, NC, as a professor of economics during the 1962 to 1963 school year and, after interviewing the school administrator, they learned the following information:

When Stapleton applied for work at this college, he stated that he was seeking a permanent position because he wanted his wife with him and further stated that he missed her dreadfully. Shortly after he began teaching at the school, information was received indicating that he was a homosexual and was questioned about this matter and confronted with information that he was forced to resign his position at the Northeast Louisiana State College in Monroe, because of his homosexual tendencies. Stapleton denied being involved in Monroe and stated that he was not a homosexual.

Stapleton expressed desire to change various policies in his department, which was not agreeable to the college officials. For this reason, the school requested Stapleton's resignation effective at the end of the 1962 spring semester.

These F.B.I. agents were advised that the college had no actual knowledge of evidence of homosexual acts committed by Stapleton while instructing at that college.

F.B.I. agents at Virginia verify E.R. Stapleton was employed as a professor at Frederick College Portsmouth, VA, during the school year 61-62. He signed a new contract to teach there during 1962 but resigned voluntarily on June 13th, 1962, after expressing that he wanted a change of employment.

Information furnished that these agents received that Stapleton had no known close friends, lived beyond his means of income at the college and no information concerning his sexual habits.

F.B.I. agents at Commerce Texas have verified that E.R. Stapleton was employed as a professor at East Texas State College Commerce, TX. Beginning in the fall term of 1958 and ending the spring term of 1961. Stapleton was discharged from his duties because of homosexual tendencies. This action was based on accusations by students and inappropriate approaches to workers and to various faculty members.

F.B.I. agents at Monroe, LA, have verified that E.R. Stapleton was employed at as a professor at Northeast Louisiana State College beginning in the fall of 1955 until the spring of 1957, information was received indicating that a complaint was made to the Sheriff's Office, Monroe, LA, accusing Stapleton of being homosexual, and Stapleton was arrested at his apartment. Investigation correlated information received in the complaint and Stapleton agreed to resign his position at the college and leave the state of Louisiana if no arrests were made.

Info on Ray's activities
in Superior, WI

Supplement #57
City of Superior, WI November 13th, 1963. Attention W. A. Tutor Sergeant.

In answer to your inquiry regarding the above-named subject, please be advised as follows of our meager findings. We have been unable to obtain any information that would establish this individual as an active homosexual. There have been suspicions of it by some of his former associates, but only due to his feminine actions. In this matter, we have no further investigation and if anything develops you will be promptly informed.

Neighbors in the apartment house of his former residence state that Stapleton was very quiet, lived alone, returned home most of the time when not at his teaching job and associated very little with the others in the building. Others in the apartment building are retired and active female teachers and businesswomen, several in all. These that would be worthy of contacting state that, after Stapleton received information about his wife's death, he became very emotional and cried a great deal of the time after returning from your area. After the funeral, he told other apartment residents that it was the opinion of the police in your area, that his wife witnessed a burglary next door to the laundromat she was in, and that the burglars apparently took her out and murdered her because she knew "too much" about their activities of that night. Stapleton further has stated that he wanted to bring his daughter back to Superior with him, but the F.B.I. advised him against such action and that is why he quit his job here and would return to Arkansas to be with her as she would need him after this thing happened in the family.

Clara Florence Lowery Bartley

❖❖

Journal type entry form Clarita's mother, Ruby's sister.

This entry gives insight into the atmosphere in the home in the days immediately following Ruby's disappearance. Emotions were fragile and to say everyone was scared would be an understatement.

Dated: Tuesday night, October 15ᵗʰ, 1963

Doctor Benson called and said we should get Clarita out of the house immediately and into the dormitory. He didn't give definite reasons but repeated this several times, very urgently. My fears had been growing all the time and I didn't want Daddy (Daddy being Clarita's father) to wait until the weekend. He called Bob Scott, who was happy to take Daddy to Searcy. (the water tank is on the truck for having to haul water for cattle) and I needed the car to get to school. Doctor B said Ray had been questioned 3 hours and Mary

Claire and Clarita 1 1/2 hours each. The police were unhappy with Clarita's answers. She said to Daddy later she told all the truth she knew but didn't know much. The police felt she had been told and threatened as to what to say.

Daddy and Bobby got to Searcy very early. Doctor Benson wasn't up but got up immediately when he knew Daddy was there. At first, he was hesitant about talking in front of Bobby until he knew Bobby's concern and relationship with us. Then he told how the police were very suspicious of Ray. He admitted to the police that he is a homosexual. Even boasted about it. All the men at college knew of this it seems, long ago. Daddy and Bobby talked with the police too. They have court orders to go into all of Ruby's finances, checks too. Even had some of her correspondence from Ray. They have records of the many checks Ray wrote at one time until Ruby stopped all payment of his checks. He had her account nearly depleted. He had checks up in the 100, some smaller, $50-$150.00, etc. Many were to the transients who had called from Lubbock. They had record of phone calls Ray had made for months. The men he called often were criminals. Sometimes they called him at home, but he wouldn't talk there. He would leave and go to a pay phone and call them, paying for the call himself. Some calls as far as California. Many checks were to them. I don't believe Ruby knew what these people were or what he must have told her about them, but one time Ruby and Ray went to Little Rock shopping and one of these two men were along. Ray put him up in one of Little Rock's best hotels, paid for it. The other man joined them, coming over from Morrilton.

Ray went to church Sunday the 13th, the first time he'd been in years. He was very cheerful and slightly joking. Not at all a grieving person. He insinuated that Ruby had been having affairs with other men, and one finally caught up with her. Also, that if she came back, he intended to have her committed to an asylum. He told the police of his dislike for her, and Mary Claire told them she hated her mother. I think he has either influenced and poisoned her mind or she has inherited his tendencies, which may account for her attitudes about dating and her "moods."

When Daddy went to the house to see Clarita, Mary Claire hugged him and kissed his cheek, glad to see him. Clarita sobbed for 20 minutes in Daddy's arms. Daddy whispered to her that he had come to take her to the dormitory or bring her home. She said she couldn't, (very insistent). The police wanted to get Mary Claire and Ray away and have Clarita look through the house for some threatening letters Ray had written her. Daddy refused to let her do this. Said the police could get warrants and do their own searching. Ray was very hateful when he met daddy and Bobby and slammed the door to the dining room saying they had to have their breakfast. Daddy and Bobby left to talk to Doctor Benson and when they returned, Ray flew into a rage. Clarita had told him she was moving. Ray told Daddy that he told us over the phone he didn't want us there, that Clarita was welcome, the only ray of sunshine they had. She was no bother, etc., and refused to let her move. He was so insulting Daddy went outside to keep from listening to his abuse. Ray Baker and Ralph McCluggage have been staying at Ray's since Ruby's disappearance. Jerry and Bobby helped get Clarita's things to the car where Daddy was. Actually, Bobby stayed with Clarita and Jerry carried the things because as long as Bobby was there, Ray wouldn't go where he was. In the meantime, Ray began phoning the dorm mother, Doctor B, etc. to prevent Daddy's taking Clarita away. Clarita is now in the dormitory, Daddy said. She was able to smile and act as if she were freed of some terrible weight. Doctor Benson praised her enthusiastically. Said she was the most popular well-liked girl there. A wonderful girl, student and Christian. He has ordered that <u>no one</u> should see Clarita without his permission as he feels she needs protection to that extent. Under no circumstance is Ray to see her and he will stop Mary Claire's visits if they become too frequent so that it might seem that she is acting as an agent for Uncle Ray.

When the purpose of Daddy's being there was known and Ray began his tirade, Mary Claire began talking abusive too. Practically an echo of Ray, she told Clarita she hoped they could be friends even if the families weren't. Doctor Benson said Glen Dewey was the only one who showed any sincere concern, that he is very grieved at Ruby's disappearance. Bobby said that since a week has passed since Rudy's disappearance the Lindbergh Law is automatically, in effect, and the F.B.I. could be acted now. Until now they've been in touch with the F.B.I. but could be activated now. They've been in touch with what police are doing, but not actually engaged in the work. Ray had been interviewed on TV. He sat there smiling and jolly. People who knew the show said he didn't seem unhappy about things. Ray even called Sharon Wilson to get to keep Clarita from moving.

End of entry

Karl Karash

❖❖

Supplement #28
The following information was furnished to F.B.I. agents at Lubbock, TX on October 10th, 1963.

Karl Herman Karash, #53-13th Street, Jamestown, New York, was interviewed in the Lubbock city jail. He was advised he did not have to make a statement and any statement he made could be used against him in court. He was advised of his right to consult an attorney before making a statement.

Karash stated he first met Doctor E.R. Stapleton, Assistant Professor of Economics, Appalachian State Teachers College, Boone, NC, in April 1963, when he was hitchhiking from Jamestown, NY to Asheville, NC to join his friend Gray Frank Chandler. He explained he first met Chandler in 1959 in Amarillo, TX, and with the exception of a few weeks, had been traveling throughout the United States with Chandler since that time. He explained he and Chandler separated about the 1st of April, when he traveled to Jamestown to visit relatives, and Chandler traveled to Asheville to see his aunt.

Karash advised about April 10th, 1963, he was hitchhiking and at Christiansburg, Virginia, E.R. Stapleton drove up to him in a 1959 "Burnt Rose Cadillac." Stapleton inquired where he was going, and he informed him of his trip to Asheville. Stapleton then invited him to ride to Boone, North Carolina with him, and he first refused as he did not want to be stranded in a small town during the nighttime. Stapleton then invited him to spend the night with him at his home in Boone stating "Oh stay with me. I could just love you to death."

He advised, "I immediately recognized Doctor Stapleton as a homosexual as he had all the characteristics of one and anyone who has hitchhiked as much as 10 miles, knows that only homosexuals drive pink Cadillacs and pick up hitchhikers." He rode with Stapleton to his home in Boone, NC and spent four days in Stapleton's house. Although Stapleton had a large two-bedroom house, he only had one bed and they slept together. During the four days he was in Stapleton's home, they engaged in homosexual acts on two occasions. At the end of the fourth day, Stapleton gave him $10, purchased a bus ticket for him and informed him he would have to leave as he was expecting someone.

Karash stated Stapleton informed him he received a phone call from Jack (last name unknown) a sailor who had just been discharged in Norfolk, Virginia, informing him Jack was enroute to Boone to live with Stapleton. Stapleton claimed that Jack had lived with him before and was a homosexual and would "be jealous if he finds you here." Stapleton did not further identify Jack and he did not furnish a description.

Karash stated he then traveled to Asheville, NC, where he contacted Chandler and after staying in Asheville two days, he and Chandler hitchhiked to Knoxville, TN, then to Little Rock, AR. He called Stapleton from Little Rock, who invited him to return to Boone, NC. He did not advise Stapleton he was traveling with Chandler. He and Chandler hitchhiked to Boone and arrived there about the first week in May 1963. He contacted Stapleton, who was having a tire repaired at a local station, and he invited them to stay with him. During the nine days they lived with Stapleton, Chandler slept with Stapleton, and he slept by himself after advising Stapleton this was his wish. During this nine-day period, he engaged in a homosexual act on one occasion with Stapleton, and although he did not witness such acts between Stapleton and Chandler, he feels such acts transpired.

While in Stapleton's home, he informed them his wife taught at Harding College in Searcy, AR, and that he had formerly taught there about two years previous. He left Searcy as he became disgusted with his wife and wanted to love men. He told them he formerly taught near Norfolk, VA, the previous year. He informed them after receiving the telephone call from Jack, a recently discharged sailor, he drove to Bristol, VA, to meet Jack, only to learn he had gotten drunk and did not show up. Stapleton identified one Damon Dean Barnes, a construction worker on a dormitory being built on the campus at Appalachian State Teachers College, as being a homosexual. Barnes lived with Stapleton, and Stapleton told him and Chandler he had engaged in homosexual acts with Barnes. He has no further information concerning Barnes or his whereabouts.

Karash advised after living with Stapleton nine days, Stapleton drove him and Chandler to Roanoke, VA, where he gave them some money and paid their room rent in the Earl Hotel. He and Chandler were enroute to Philadelphia, and Stapleton acted as though he was concerned over them obtaining jobs. After Stapleton returned to Boone, he called Chandler at the Earl Hotel and asked Chandler to ditch Karl and return to live with Stapleton in Boone. He advised Chandler wanted to return to Boone due to the choice atmosphere and living with the good doctor. He and Chandler hitchhiked to Philadelphia, PA, where they sought work. Chandler called Stapleton about the middle of June, and Stapleton offered to wire Chandler money if Chandler had ditched Karash and Chandler replied he had; Stapleton then wired $50.00 to Chandler via Western Union to pay his transportation to Boone. He and Chandler used these funds to live on while seeking employment.

He stated Stapleton later told Chandler he was highly disappointed that Chandler did not return to Boone and live with him as he had ordered a large spray of flowers from a local florist, pinned a note on them, reading "Welcome Home Gray, Love Doc" and had placed them on a table in his home in Boone. He stated Chandler obtained this $50 only after promising Stapleton he had returned to Boone as soon as he could make the trip. He has the card described in his effects at the star hotel, as Stapleton gave this card to Chandler in August, 1963.

He and Chandler then hitchhiked to Los Angeles, CA and stayed in the Cecil Hotel and other small places in Los Angeles. About July 18-20, 1963, he and Chandler were broke and they decided to call Stapleton at his home in Searcy, AR. Stapleton had informed them earlier he planned to seek a teaching position in Southern California, and they expected to hear he was in California teaching. They intended to contact Stapleton to obtain funds. Stapleton answered his telephone in Searcy, and Chandler told him he had gotten drunk and was thrown in jail, which prevented him from making the trip to Boone. Stapleton again begged Chandler to come to Arkansas and remain until he could obtain a teaching job in "some larger town" and take Chandler to live with him. Chandler then promised to make the trip to Arkansas if Stapleton would wire the funds. He wired $50 one day, called the following day, and upon being informed by Chandler that $50 wasn't enough, wired $100 the third day. Chandler again assured Stapleton he "had ditched me" and was traveling alone.

Karl advised he and Chandler hitchhiked to Morrilton, AR where Chandler called Stapleton, who came to Morrilton and picked up Chandler. He remained in Morrilton while Stapleton drove Chandler to Beebe, AR and paid for his motel room. The following day, Stapleton drove to Beebe, picked up Chandler and drove from Little Rock where he paid two weeks rent in a hotel for Chandler. He spent one night in Morrilton, hitchhiked to Little Rock with one Joseph Worm, employee of the Double R Florist, 1200 West Main, Jacksonville, AR and lived with Worm, a homosexual, for about one week. He and Chandler were in contact with each other, and Chandler stayed in the Capitol Hotel across from the Trailways Bus Depot. Stapleton gave Chandler at least $40 on one occasion and took Chandler with him to Pensacola, FL where Stapleton attempted to obtain a teaching job in a junior college. Chandler later told him that he spent the night at the Holiday Inn, Jackson, Mississippi, on the way to Pensacola and on the return trip to Little Rock.

After staying in Little Rock for about a week, Karash hitchhiked to Nashville, TN, where he visited "friends." He declined to identify these friends. He then returned to Little Rock and contacted Chandler, who by this time was "disgusted with the Doctor as he did not like waiting around in Little Rock in all the heat." Although Chandler knew Stapleton was to visit him in the hotel that day, he and Chandler rode a bus to Memphis, TN, and after spending one night there, hitchhiked to Nashville, TN through Moline, Illinois; Davenport, Iowa; Kansas City, MO; Wichita, KS; into Amarillo, TX; then to Lubbock.

Karash advised he and Chandler arrived in Lubbock, TX Saturday, October 5th, 1963, at about 11:00 a.m. They attended a movie and spent the night at the Salvation Army. October 6th, 1963, they contacted Joseph Fasel, Assistant Rector, St. Paul's. Episcopal

Church, 1510 Avenue X and obtained food and lodging for one night. Fasel called the Saint Francis Hotel and guaranteed their rent for one night. On October 7th, 1963, the manager of the hotel called Fasel who extended the offer for one more night. They remained in the Saint Francis Hotel until October 8th when they moved to the Salvation Army. After spending the night there, they contacted the business manager, at the First Christian Church, who told them that the church owned the Star Hotel, and they could stay two nights in that hotel. They spent the night of October 9th, 1963, in the Star Hotel. On Monday October 7th, 1963, they each sold a pint of blood at the Southwest Blood bank, Lubbock.

On October 10th, 1963 they were broke and again decided to call Doctor E.R. Stapleton, Searcy, AR, and ask him for money. They walked from the Star Hotel to the Broadway Drug Store, located at Broadway and College Ave, Lubbock, where Chandler placed a collect call under the name of Frank Stevens, as he was afraid the call would not be accepted if Mrs. Stapleton answered the phone. They realized Stapleton would recognize Chandler's voice if he talked and therefore would not accept the call. He remained near the phone booth and could hear Chandler tell Stapleton he was in Lubbock, TX, broke and needed money. He stated Chandler's conversation was as follows. "Hello Doctor. Do you know who this is? This is Gray. I thought I would call and see what you were doing. I did not want to use another name, but I was afraid you would not accept this call in my name." After that Stapleton talked but he could not hear what was said.

Chandler then stated "I am in Lubbock looking for a job. I am making this call from a drug store located across the street from the College in Lubbock. I do not have much money and am looking for work. I was wondering if you could help us a little bit?" He stated Chandler did not demand money from Stapleton and did not threaten him in any manner. He did not hear Chandler use any words similar to "that does not leave me but one alternative" or any conversation where the word alternative was used. He stated the conversation lasted some 30 minutes, and he and Chandler were arrested by Lieutenant Ferguson of the Lubbock police, who took the phone and talked to Stapleton.

Karash repeated neither he nor Chandler demanded money from Stapleton or demanded that he send the money. He repeated

Chandler did not tell Stapleton he, Karash, was in Lubbock, and there was no reason for Stapleton to know he was in Lubbock.

Karash stated the first he learned that Mrs. Stapleton was missing from Searcy was when he was questioned about it by Lieutenant Ferguson of the Police Department, Lubbock, TX. He stated he has never met Mrs. Stapleton, did not see or contact Stapleton from August 12th, 1963, until October 10th, 1963, and has not been in the state of Arkansas since August 12th, 1963. He has not read anything about the disappearance of Mrs. Stapleton and knows nothing and would not want to kidnap or harm her.

He stated although Stapleton informed him he could no longer stand to live with his wife, he does not believe Stapleton would harm his wife and can offer no suggestion as to her whereabouts. Stapleton informed him he has a son in Searcy and a daughter attending Vanderbilt University in Tennessee. Stapleton claimed his wife had a doctorate in English from Iowa and Oklahoma Universities. Karash furnished the following description of himself. He states that he was discharged from the military as homosexual in 1957.

Gray Frank Chandler
❖

Supplement #29
The following information was furnished to F.B.I. Agents at Lubbock, Texas, on October 10th, 1963.

Gray F. Chandler, 35 Proverd road, Asheville, North Carolina, was interviewed in the Lubbock County Jail. He was advised he did not have to make a statement and any statement he made could be used against him in a court of law. He was advised of his right to consult an attorney before making a statement.

He advised he first met Karl Herman Karash in Amarillo, Texas in about January 1959. They first met in a bar and have been traveling throughout the United States since that time with short breaks when Karash visited his mother in Jamestown, New York, and he visited his aunt in Asheville, North Carolina. He stated they hitchhiked around the country staying in Salvation Army houses, Young Men's Christian Associations hotels when they can obtain rooms from local churches or funds they occasionally earn from odd jobs. They have not held permanent jobs since 1959 and have no jobs now.

About the middle of April 1963, Karash hitchhiked to Asheville, North Carolina, to rejoin Chandler, after spending three weeks in Jamestown, New York. Karash told him while enroute to Asheville, he had obtained a ride with one Dr. Stapleton, Assistant Professor of Economics, Appalachian State Teachers College, Boone, North Carolina, and had spent four days in Stapleton's home in Boone. He and Karash began hitchhiking and traveled to Johnson City, Tennessee; Columbus, Mansfield, and Lancaster, Ohio; Indianapolis, Indiana; Danville and Peoria, Illinois; Davenport, Iowa; and Little Rock, Arkansas. From Little Rock, they traveled to Boone, North Carolina, where Karash contacted Stapleton. They spent nine days in Stapleton's house, and he slept with Stapleton during his stay in his home. He and Stapleton engaged in homosexual acts while he was in his house.

During the nine days he and Karash were in Stapleton's home, he informed them he obtained a doctorate in Economics and his wife had a doctorate in English and taught at Harding College, Searcy, Arkansas.

Stapleton told him he has had homosexual tendencies for the past 25 years, but "controlled them until I finished my education and raised my two children." Stapleton stated he taught at Harding College until about two years ago and left Searcy as he was disgusted with his wife and could no longer stand her. He openly expressed his desire to "love men" and openly mentioned having affairs with men while teaching one year in a small college near Norfolk, Virginia, and with men in Boone, Carolina. He mentioned "being intimate" with a sailor just discharged from the Navy at Norfolk, Virginia, whose first name is Jack and stated Jack had lived in his house with him. Another homosexual mentioned by Stapleton was a man in Boone, who "is some kind of religious worker" who writes poems and goes around reading them to groups of people. Stapleton claimed one Damon Dean Barnes, a construction worker employed on the new dormitory at Appalachian State College, was a homosexual and had lived with him in his house in Boone. He stated he did not meet any of these men and can furnish no descriptions.

Chandler advised when he and Karash decided to hitchhike to Philadelphia, Pennsylvania, Stapleton attempted to persuade him to remain in Boone until he finished that term of teaching. Stapleton promised he would obtain a teaching job in some large town, and they could live together "without talk." He declined and Stapleton drove him and Karash to Roanoke, Virginia, where he paid their hotel bill at the Earl Hotel and gave each $10. Stapleton returned to Boone, but the following morning called him at the hotel and again begged him to return to Boone and live with him. Stapleton claimed he had called his (Chandler's) aunt in Asheville, North Carolina, and "had checked on me and found me to be ok." Stapleton requested that he take Karash to Philadelphia, "ditch him, and come back here and live with me." He and Karash hitchhiked to Philadelphia and about the first part of June 1963, were broke and needed funds. He called Stapleton in Boone, told him he had "ditched Karl," and if Stapleton wired him some money, he would travel to Boone and live with him. Stapleton wired him $50 that day.

He and Karash remained in Philadelphia for about another two weeks, then hitchhiked to Los Angeles, California. About July 19 or 20, 1963, he placed a collect call to Stapleton in Searcy, Arkansas, fully expecting to be informed by Mrs. Stapleton that Dr. Stapleton was teaching in some college in California. Stapleton had expressed his intention of going to California to obtain a position and he thought he could contact him there for money. He advised, Stapleton answered the phone and informed him he made a trip to California but did not like it there and had returned to Searcy while trying to obtain a teaching job. Chandler told Stapleton he had gotten drunk, thrown in jail, after receiving the money in Philadelphia, and was ashamed to contact Stapleton after he got out of jail.

He stated he promised Stapleton he would come to Arkansas and wait in Little Rock until Stapleton could obtain a job in some college if Stapleton would send him some money. Stapleton inquired if Karash was with him, and he told him he was not. Stapleton then wired $50 and wanted him to hurry to Arkansas. The following day he called, stating he was sending more money as he did not want him to hitchhike as it would take him too long. Three days later Stapleton wired him $100, and he and Karash used these funds to live on. They then decided to travel to Arkansas, "and I might live with the Doctor long enough to get enough money to get back into the radio business." He advised he formerly worked a radio announcer and thought "the money Dr. Stapleton would give me would enable me to get new clothes and put myself in shape to get a good job in radio."

He told him he would visit him in Little Rock in two days. He met a friend and been staying at the YMCA with a man he met, and they decided to leave Little Rock as Stapleton was unable to obtain a job. Stapleton said he had a job offer in Queensboro, Kentucky; Edinburg, Texas; South Dakota; but had not obtained a position. He added, he was too hot waiting around in that old hotel room for him.

Chandler advised about August 11th or 12th, 1963, he and Karash left Little Rock /and traveled to Memphis, Tennessee, where they spent two nights in a hotel across the street from the Trailways Bus Station. They used funds supplied for their transportation and lodging. They hitch hiked to; Hopkinsville, Kentucky; Evansville, Indiana; into Illinois, Oklahoma, and then into Amarillo, Texas.

On October 5, 1963, traveled to Lubbock, Texas where they spent the night at the Salvation Army. On October 6th they contacted Joseph Fasel assistant reverend at Episcopal Church, who agreed to pay one night's lodging at the St. Francis hotel in Lubbock. They checked into the hotel and contacted Dr. Golightly, West Texas Hospital, and Golightly wrote a prescription for him. He stated his fee and when they informed him, they did not have the money for the prescription Golightly instructed his nurse to call the Drug store and have the bill sent to him. In attempting to obtain his prescription there was some misunderstanding as the druggist wanted Golightly to confirm their story.

On October 7th, 1963, Karash contacted the business manager of the church and informed him of his trouble. This man attempted to cover the prescription left at the drugstore where they would bill the church. He filled the prescription for Karash who then had it filled at Walgreens. They later went to the Southwest blood bank where they each sold blood for 5 dollars each.

Lieutenant James Fergerson

❖❖❖

Lubbock Police Department covering arrest
of Karash and Chandler

Supplement #30 and #31
The following information was furnished to F.B.I. Agents at
Lubbock, Texas, on October 11th, 1963.

James Fergerson, advised at about 11a.m., October 10th, 1963, had received a phone call from Benson Robbins, Deputy Sheriff, Searcy, Arkansas, advising him one Gray Frank Chandler was then in the process of making a phone call to E.R. Stapleton, Searcy, Arkansas, from a phone, Porter2-9676, in Lubbock, Texas, and Chandler was demanding money from Stapleton. He advised Robbins furnished the telephone number from which Chandler was calling and determined it to be located in the Broadway Drug Store, Broadway at College Avenue, Lubbock.

Fergerson advised at 11:10 a.m. he arrested Gray Frank Chandler as he was talking over the phone from the Broadway Drug and after arresting Chandler took the phone and talked to a man who identified himself to be E.R. Stapleton, Searcy, AR. He advised he also arrested Karl Herman Karash who was standing near the phone booth as Chandler talked to Stapleton.

Chandler and Karash claim they have known Stapleton since April 1963, having met him in Boone, NC, and Chandler claimed he called Stapleton to ask for money. Chandler denied demanding money from Stapleton. Chandler and Karash denied knowledge that Mrs. E.R. Stapleton was missing from her home in Searcy, Arkansas.

He advised Chandler and Karash claimed they arrived in Lubbock on Saturday, October 5th, 1963, spent that night at the Salvation Army, contacted the Reverend Joseph Fasel, Episcopal Church, who agreed to pay for two night's lodging in the St. Francis hotel, Lubbock, and stayed in that hotel the nights of October 6 and

7, 1963.

On October 8, 1963, they returned to the Salvation Army and spent the night there. On October 9th, 1963, they contacted the Business Manager, Broadway Church of Christ, who placed them in the Star Hotel, 16th and College Ave, Lubbock, Texas. They claimed they have been in Lubbock continually since October 5, 1963.

He advised he has verified the information furnished by Chandler and Karash in that they did spend the nights listed in the Salvation Army, St. Francis, and Star Hotel.

Supplement #31,

Lieutenant, Lubbock Police Department, made available a black wallet which he identified as being the property of Karl Herman Karash and having been on Karash's person when he arrested him at Broadway Drugstore in Lubbock on October 10th, 1963.

This wallet contained items identified in part as follows. Draft Registration card Local Board 92 Village Hall, Fredonia, NY, duplicate issue to Karl Herman Karash: 3118 Terrace Ave, Lakewood, New York. Selective Service number is 050306632. Card of the Double R Florist, 1200 W Main Jacksonville, AR 1515 W 8th 23126 Yu 22327. Slip of paper bearing: Doctor E.R. Stapleton 206 Cornell. Council St. Boone, NC CH-929 Phone 264-8777, Area code 704. Hotel receipts of the Cecil Hotel, town not given, dated July 11th, 13th, and 15th, 1963 in the name of Chandler Karash.

William Key

❖❖

**Manager, Salvation Army, Lubbock, Texas, verifying
alibi of Karash and Chandler**

Supplement #34

William Key, manager, Salvation Army, 112 Dash 17th St. advised the records of his organization show that Karl H Karash and Gray F Chandler were admitted on October 5th, 1963, after 5:00 p.m. and were locked into the building for the night. They left the following morning shortly after 6:00 a.m. They were readmitted on October 8th, in 1963 and Karash was listed as being fifth in line for a bed, he believes he must have arrived at the shelter by 5:00 p.m. Chandler was listed as being 9th for a bed. They were awakened at 5:30 a.m. on October 9th, 1963, fed, and released.

Key advised no one has permitted to enter or leave the building after once checking in for the day, and both Karash and Chandler were confined to his shelter on the night of October 8th, 1963. The above information was furnished to F.B.I. agents at Lubbock, TX on October 11th, 1963.

Bess Summers

❖❖

Manager, Star Hotel, Lubbock, Texas verifying
alibi of Karash and Chandler

Supplement #35
The following information was furnished to F.B.I. agents at Lubbock, TX on October 14th, 1963.

Mrs. Bess Summers, Manager, Star Hotel, 1515 College Ave, advised on October 9th, 1963, she received a telephone call from

Mr. Johnny Davis, First Christian church informing her that he was sending two men to the hotel to spend two nights. The church owns the hotel, and no charges were to be collected from the men. She advised at about 2:00 p.m. that day, two men identified to her as Karash and Chandler, came to the hotel and told her they would obtain their clothes and return later that evening. At about 10:00 p.m. they were returned and were assigned rooms 7 and 8. She stated Chandler did not have any luggage, but Karash had Chandler's clothes and shaving kit in his small canvas bag. She turned this bag into to Agents Stevens and Elliot.

Karash's hotel room contents as described by Bess Summers

Supplement #32
The following information was furnished to F.B.I. Agents at Lubbock, Texas, on October 11, 1963:

A small, zippered traveling case was obtained by a Mrs. Bess Summers, manager, Star Hotel, 1515 College Avenue, bearing the name, "K.H. Karash." A search of this bag revealed it contained men's clothing, two sizes, and correspondence addressed to Karl Karash and to Gray F. Chandler. The following items were found in this bag.

Receipt- Capitol Hill Hotel, Little Rock, Arkansas, dated July 28th, 1963, Room 400. To G.F. Chandler, marked "rent 7-28 to 8-14---$18.00, tax.34 Fan $1.0, total $19.54.

Small envelope marked "To Gray" containing a small photograph of a middle-aged white male, wearing glasses and a thin mustache, and balding, with a high forehead, and a small card bearing the words, "To Gray with All My Love, Doc."

An envelope addressed to Mr. Gray F. Chandler, The Capitol Hill Hotel, Room 400 Little Rock, Arkansas with the return address of E.R. Stapleton, 910 East Center Avenue, Searcy, Arkansas, 72143. Postmarked at Searcy, Arkansas at 6:00 a.m. July 31st, 1963, the envelope contained a letter dated July 30th, 1963, headed, "Dear Gray," and two paragraphs of this letter reads as follows:

"What have you been doing Gray? What about the radio work? Any possibility? I don't know why I'm asking you these questions, for I don't expect you to reply. It just seems natural to ask. Mrs. Stapleton and I expect to come to Little Rock on Friday afternoon of this week. We shall want you to eat with us somewhere and I will call you early Friday morning about details. Do go with us and don't be nervous. Just be your usual sweet self. And let us both enjoy you together. Take care of yourself now. We will be seeing you real, real soon. Your friend Doc."

A letter addressed to Karl Karash, General Delivery, Davenport, Iowa from the First Methodist Church, Burlington, Iowa, headed, "Dear Karl and Gray" and signed by G. Dempster Yinger Minister. This letter expresses willingness to assist sorrow over "depressing difficulties" and hopes that they will make progress. The envelope bears a date of delivery of September 7th, 1963.

A bottle of salve bearing a prescription of Walgreens Drug Lubbock, TX number 111602, price $1.50, reflecting it was issued to by Dr. Golightly on October 6th, 1963, for Mr. Karash.

L.H. Bridges

❖❖

Manager, St. Francis Hotel, Lubbock, Texas, verifying alibi of Karash and Chandler

Supplement #33.
The following information was furnished to F.B.I. agents at Lubbock, TX on October 11th, 1963.

L.H. Bridges Manager, Saint Francis Hotel, 901 Texas Ave, advised on Sunday, October 6th, 1963, Joseph Fasel, Rector, Saint Paul's Episcopal Church, Lubbock, called him and guaranteed payment of one night's lodging for Karl Karash and Gray F. Chandler and issued a requisition for free meals for these two at Jimmy's Cafe on Avenue H.

Karash and Chandler checked into the hotel room 305, and on

October 7th, 1963, were in and out of their room several times. He contacted Reverend Fasel on October 7th, 1963, who agreed to pay for another night's lodging. Karash and Chandler stayed in room 305 that day and night and left the hotel Tuesday morning, October 8th, 1963. They had no visitors and made no telephone calls.

James Douglas Daugherty

❖

Supplement #36
The following information was furnished to F.B.I. agents at Dallas,
TX on October 18th, 1963. James Douglas Daughtry, 1000 N.
Marsalis apt #5, was informed that he did not have to furnish any
statement at all, that anything he said could be used against him in
court, and that he had the right to confer with an attorney any time
he so desired. No threats or promises were made to him. He
furnished the following information.

He was born July 12th, 1943, at Myrtle Springs, TX. He is a truck driver by occupation but has been employed as a dock hand by Merchants Fast Motor Freight, 1440 Oak Lawn Ave, Dallas since about August 21st, 1963. He is presently residing at the above address with his common law wife Louise.

About four years ago, while at Commerce, Texas, he met Doctor E.R. Stapleton who was employed as an instructor at East Texas State College, Commerce, Texas. Soon thereafter, he began permitting Dr. Stapleton to commit unnatural sex acts with him. And since that time, has been in frequent contact with Stapleton when similar unnatural sex acts have taken place.

In early April 1963, he visited Dr. Stapleton at Boone, NC, where Stapleton was an instructor at Appalachian State College. On this visit, Stapleton paid $1000 down payment on a 1963 Chevrolet which was purchased from Andrews Chevrolet INC., Boone, NC. The balance was financed for Daugherty through the General Motors, Winston Salem, NC.

From Boone, he went to Los Angeles, CA where he subsequently met Louise, his present common law wife. While they were residing together at 2749 San Matino, Los Angeles, Doctor Stapleton visited him for approximately 6 days during the latter part of May and early part of June 1963. He stayed in a room in the apartment building where they were residing and later moved to a downtown hotel room. During this visit, Stapleton gave him a $750 personal check drawn on a Wolfe City, Texas bank.

He last saw Doctor Stapleton approximately five weeks ago at Texarkana, TX, after Stapleton had called him in Dallas and asked him to meet Stapleton at Texarkana. Daugherty took his common law wife with him and met Stapleton at the railroad station. The three of them had dinner together during which time Stapleton discussed sending Daugherty to school, and Stapleton was to finance Daugherty through college. During this visit, Stapleton gave him another checking amount of $250 dollars, also drawn on the Wolfe City Bank. Since he has known Stapleton, Stapleton has owned a 1959 Cadillac, which he was still driving at the Texarkana meeting.

On October 9th, 1963, he received a Western Union Telegraph from Superior, WI dated October 9th, 1963, at 11:11 a.m., Central Standard Time which advised as follows. "Call, Area code 501 Searcy, collect, early Thursday morning, E.R. Stapleton." Daugherty made available the above-described telegraph.

Daugherty's common law wife Louise left him September 27th, 1963, and stated she was returning to Los Angeles by bus to see her 14-year-old daughter who resided there with her father.

On the evening of October 9th, 1963, Daugherty also receives a letter from his wife stating she was agreeable to coming back to live with him. At approximately 8:15 a.m. on October 10th, 1963, he called Stapleton in Searcy, AR collect, at which time Stapleton advised that his wife was missing, that no one knew her whereabouts, and that the F.B.I. was investigating the case. He stated he had arrived the previous evening in Searcy by plane from Superior, WI. Stapleton furnished no details concerning the mysterious disappearance of his wife. Stapleton requested that Daugherty come to Searcy and drive him back to Superior, WI at which time Daugherty replied that it would be impossible to do so before the weekend of October 13th, 1963, since his brother had driven his 1963 Chevrolet to Pennsylvania and would not be back until the following weekend. Stapleton replied that would be perfectly satisfactory. At that time, Stapleton further inquired if Louise was still in California, and when Daugherty informed Stapleton that she was returning the next day, Stapleton became angry and requested that he cancel any future plans of financing of Daugherty's education and contacting him, and that it would be unnecessary for him to drive Stapleton back to Wisconsin.

Daugherty stated he did not believe that Stapleton was capable of doing bodily harm to Mrs. Stapleton and had never at any time heard him discuss doing any harm to her. Daugherty is not acquainted with any associates of Stapleton and has never met Mrs. Stapleton. He denied knowledge of anyone who might be responsible for Stapleton's disappearance.

Louise Marcum

❖

Supplement #38.

Louise Cyrus Marcum, who resides at 1000 N Marsalis, Dallas, TX with her common law husband James Douglas Daugherty, furnished F.B.I. agents at Dallas with the following information.

She has met Doctor E.R. Stapleton on three or four occasions, always with her common law husband and stated that she suspected Stapleton was a homosexual. However, James Douglas Daugherty had not discussed this matter with her. She was aware that Stapleton has given Daugherty large sums of money on various occasions, and Stapleton visited with her and Daugherty in California during this past summer.

Louise Marcum met Daugherty in Los Angeles during May 1963, and traveled with him to Dallas, TX, where they now reside.

On September 27th, 1963, she traveled by bus to Los Angeles, CA and lived with Ruth Marcum at 924 N Kingsley Dr. Apt. 4, in that city until October 11th, 1963, on which date she took a plane from Los Angeles to Dallas, TX. During her stay in California, she was employed at the Kingsley Manner, a Nursing Home, 1035 Kingsley Dr., Los Angeles, CA, from October 1st through October 10th, 1963, and knew nothing of Mrs. Stapleton's disappearance until October 11th, 1963, when she arrived in Dallas and was told this information by Daugherty.

Louise Marcum is described as a white female, age 30 something, is five feet one inch tall and is 110 lbs. She is married, separated, and her husband has legal custody of the two minor children.

R.T. Johnson

◆◆

**Foreman, Merchants Fast Motor Freight,
Dallas Texas, verifying Daugherty's alibi.**

Supplement #37
The following information was furnished to F.B.I. agents at Dallas, TX on October 18th, 1963.

R.T. Johnson, General Dock Foreman, Merchants Fast Motor Freight, 1440 Oak Lawn Ave., Dallas furnished the following information.

James Douglas Daugherty, 1000 N Marsalis, Dallas, is presently employed as a dockhand and has been still employed since August 21st, 1963.

Johnson made available timecards reflecting Daugherty's time on duty for the following dates.

October 7th, 1963, signed in at 12:18 p.m. and signed out for home at 10:15 p.m.

October 8th, 1963, signed in. at 12:36 p.m. and signed out for home at 9:59 p.m.

October 9th, 1963, signed in at 12:16 p.m. and signed out for home at 10:15 p.m.

October 11th, 1963, signed in at 12:16 p.m. and signed out for home at 7:31 p.m.

October 12th, 1963 (Saturday), signed in at 8:00 a.m. and signed out for home at 12:36 p.m.

Johnson advised that the time clock is in his office, and it is necessary for each employee to punch the time clock when he goes on or off duty and that he, Johnson, keeps a close check on each employee to be certain no fraud is involved in this regard. He stated he knows Daugherty has been a good employee.

Genella George

❖❖

Transmittal Secretary, Kingsley Manor, verifying alibi of Louise Marcum, Daugherty's common law wife.

Supplement #39
The following information was furnished to F.B.I. agents in Los Angeles, CA by Miss Genelia George, Transmittal Secretary, Kingsley Manor, 1055 N Kingsley Dr., Los Angeles, CA.

Louise Marcum was hired as a relief nurse at Kingsley Manor on September 30th, 1963, and worked October 1st-5th and 8th-10th, 1963.

She is the sister-in-law of Ruth Marcum who has been employed at Kingsley Manor continuously since April 1957, and she recently married Paul King; their address is now listed as 905 N Ardmore apt 1, Los Angeles, CA.

Daniel Glen Daugherty

◈◈

Supplement #40
Statement of Daniel Glen Daugherty. Route 1, Ben Wheeler, Texas

Daniel Glen Daugherty, described as a white male, dob 9-18-39. Wt.175, brown eyes and blue hair, furnished F.B.I. agents with the following information.

He is employed at Kelly-Springfield Tire CO. Chandler Highway, Tyler, Texas. Separated from his wife, Francis Ann Daugherty, who resides with her mother in Philadelphia, Pennsylvania. On the evening of October 7th, 1963, he left Ben Wheeler, Texas about 7 p.m. in a white over aqua 1963 Chevrolet Tudor Hardtop, bearing California license, and which automobile is in the property of his brother, James Douglas Daugherty. Daniel and Dewey Daugherty drove all night Monday, all day and all night Tuesday, and arrived in Philadelphia, Pennsylvania, about 8:00a.m. Wednesday, October 9th, 1963.

They lodged at the residence of Mrs. Clara Vose, 4324 Freeland Ave, Philadelphia, who is the mother-in-law of Daniel Daugherty, and while in Philadelphia bought a tire from the Penn-Jersey Auto Supply, Ridge Avenue.

Dewey and Daniel Daugherty left Philadelphia in the automobile about 10 a.m. Thursday, October 10, 1963, and traveled to Charlotte, North Carolina, where they lodged at the Catalina Motor Lodge. Daniel Daugherty visited a friend, Sue Berry, 1312 Skyway Drive, Concord, North Carolina, and on the night, they lodged at Charlotte. Both Daniel and Dewey Daugherty left Charlotte, North Carolina, about 11 a.m. Friday October 11th, 1963, and drove to Ben Wheeler Texas, arriving about 7 a.m. Saturday, October 12th, 1963.

Francis Ann Daugherty

◈◈

Supplement #42
Francis Ann Daugherty was interviewed at her mother's house,
4324 Freeland, Ave, Philadelphia, Pennsylvania.

Mrs. Daugherty was advised she did not have to furnish any information in this matter and that any statement she did make could be used in a court of law.

Mrs. Daugherty advised she is married to Daniel Daugherty, but they have not lived together since June 1963, when she returned to Philadelphia. She added that she married Daniel Daugherty in August 1961, in Elkton, Maryland, while he was in the U.S. Navy. He was discharged in August of 1962, and they lived together in Ben Wheeler, Texas until she returned to Philadelphia in June 1963.

She states she has only seen Daniel Daugherty since June 1963 and that his brother, Dewey, came to Philadelphia in October 1963. She stated they drove up in the car of their brother, Douglas Daugherty, a 1963 Chevrolet, arriving at 4324 Freeland Ave around 8 a.m. Wednesday, October 9th, 1963. She stated they visited various members of their family during the day on October 9th, and Daniel and Dewey spent the night at her mother's residence. She stated they drove to the Penn Jersey Auto Supply on Ridge Ave, near where she lives, to purchase a tire. She did not recall whether this was on October 9th or on the morning of October 10th, 1963. She said that Daniel and Dewey left to return to Ben Wheeler, Texas in the middle of the morning October 10th, 1963.

Mrs. Daugherty continued that her son Glen Curtis was born October 29, 1963, and she talked with Daniel on the telephone within a day or two of the birth of her son.

Dewey Daugherty

❖

Supplement #41
Statement of Dewey Daugherty, Myrtle Springs, Texas

Dewey Daugherty who is described as a white male, 23, 160 lbs., was interviewed by F.B.I. Agents and furnished information which corroborated that given by his brother Daniel Glenn Daugherty, concerning their travels from Ben Wheeler, Texas to Philadelphia, Pennsylvania, and return, beginning October 7, 1963, and returning October 12, 1963.

Oscar Halpern

❖

Owner Penn-Jersey Auto Store, Verifying alibi of
Dewey and Daniel Daugherty

Supplement #43
Oscar Halpern was interviewed at his store. Mr. Halpern was advised that he did not have to furnish any information and that any statement he did make could be used in a court of law.

Mr. Halpern stated they do not keep any record by which he could identify cash sale; however, if the sale involved a tire, he could perhaps locate a record of the guarantee card which would have been issued to the purchaser.

He checked records of tire guarantees issued during the month of October 1963, and located a guarantee form, which is described as a small, printed form bearing the heading, "Cordovan Nationwide Tire Service Guarantee Form." That indicates the sale on October 8th, 1963, of one tire to Daniel Daugherty, Route 1, Ben Wheeler, Texas. He stated that according to the initials on the form, this tire was sold by his brother-in-law, Morris Rochlin. He stated this was a

14 inch which sold for approximately $15.20.

He stated the original of this form would have been given to Daugherty at the time of purchase.

Morris Rochlin

◆◈◆

Employee of Penn-Jersey Auto Store, verifying alibi of Dewey and Daniel Daugherty

Supplement #44
The following information was furnished to F.B.I. agents. Morris Rochlin was interviewed at the Penn Jersey Auto Store, 6131 Ridge Avenue, where he is employed. Mr. Rochlin was advised he did not have to furnish any information in this matter and that any statement he did make could be used in a court of law.

Mr. Rochlin stated that he recalls the sale of a tire to a man from Texas. After reviewing the guarantee form which indicated the tire was sold on October 8th, 1963, he stated he feels this date correctly reflects the date of the sale, but he is not absolutely sure. He stated, for instance, that on the morning of October 9th, 1963, he may have inadvertently dated a form October 8th, 1963. He said he does not recall what day of the week this sale was on but does recall it was early in the week. He stated the tire was mounted on the car by an employee of the store at the time of purchase; he concluded that the tire was paid for in cash.

Mrs. M. Castles

◆◈◆

Bookkeeper, Catalina Motor Lodge, Charlotte, North Carolina, Verifying alibi of Danny Daugherty

Supplement #45
This information was furnished to F.B.I. agents.

Mrs. M. Castles, bookkeeper of the Catalina Motor Lodge, Wilkinson Blvd, Charlotte, NC, advised that her records reflected that registration number 78904 showed that Daniel C. Daugherty, Route One Ben Wheeler, Texas was registered in room #114 with another individual whose name was unknown. The automobile they were driving bore California license J QX956. The date of registration was October 10th, 1963. Payment was made in advance for one evening and the party of two checked out on October 11th, 1963. The room clerk put down on the registration book the name Daniel Daugherty. The amount paid for the one evening was $12.36. Mrs. Castle stated that the other individual was a white male, name unknown, who also occupied the room with Daniel Daugherty.

Mrs. Sue Edwards Lentz
◈◈

Concord, North Carolina, Verifying Alibi of Danny Daugherty (James Douglas Daugherty's brother)

Supplement #46
The following information was furnished to F.B.I. Agents:

Mrs. Sue Edwards Lentz, 1012 Skyway Drive, Concord, North Carolina, advised that Daniel Daugherty, whom she knows as Danny Daugherty, visited her home on the evening of October 10, 1963, at about 7:00 p.m. and stayed until 11 p.m. She stated that he told her that he had just traveled from Pennsylvania on his way back to Texas. She stated that he did not tell her the identity of the person with whom he was traveling, but she understood that he was driving a relative's car.

Mrs. Lentz stated that she met Daniel Daugherty at Canton, Texas, during the week of July 4th, 1963, while she was visiting her sister, Ann Sanders, and her brother-in-law, Bobby Sanders, at Myrtle Springs, Texas. She stated that Ann and Bobby Sanders actually reside about 5 miles out of Myrtle Springs. She stated that she knows nothing concerning the character and morals of Daniel Daugherty, but that in her opinion, he did not appear to have any homosexual tendencies. She stated that Daniel Daugherty had never mentioned anything to her about either Dr. Stapleton or Mrs. Stapleton.

The following information and statements are from possible suspects detectives investigated due to their previous criminal behavior and/or having committed crimes similar to Ruby's.

Detective Bob Satterwhite-Eugene Wesley Howard Info
❖❖

On November 14th, 1963, Detective Sergeant Bob Satterwhite, Little Rock Police Department, furnished the following information for consideration in the Stapleton Case.

Subject Eugene Wesley Howard was arrested on a warrant dated September 17th, 1963, charging him with obtaining money under false pretense. This case involved the subject's receiving $3100 from a friend, Mrs. Alford, 1617 Center St., Little Rock, AR. Employee of the Kroger company, 14th and Main, Little Rock. (Hendrix, the manager) who had become acquainted with the subject, experienced confidence in him and had agreed to finance his venture into the independent trucking business. After the money was furnished to the subject, he made no effort to go into business and the warrant was then issued. On September 18th, 1963, Howard had a preliminary hearing in Little Rock Municipal Court and was bound over by Judge Clover to the Pulaski County grand jury a short time later. The complaining witness wrote the Judge a letter stating that the subject had made full restitution and requested that the charge be dropped. The Little Rock police have learned that Howard has worked for the Cadillac Company of Little Rock as a car salesman and later worked for the Capital City Business School in Little Rock as a guidance counselor. He has resided at 300 W 18th St., Little Rock. The F.B.I. record for this subject indicates that he is number 242-9225, and that he has a record at Phoenix, AZ for aggravated assault, kidnapping, grand larceny of an automobile, and other charges.

Sammy Sterling Stanley

❖❖

Statement given to law enforcement by Sammy Sterling, November 10th, 1963.

I, Sammy Sterling Stanley, age 23, was off work yesterday, Saturday, left home about 7:00 p.m., drove alone to North Little Rock and stopped at several drive-ins. While driving around, I had the urge to expose myself to a woman, drove out on the highway between Jacksonville and North Little Rock, and drove up behind a foreign car with a young woman alone driving north. I passed her and drove on ahead about a mile. I stopped on the side of the road, east shoulder, got out of my car, pulled my pants and under shorts off and I stood beside my car, between the left door and the highway, while this woman drove by. I don't recall making any hand or body motions to stop this woman.

After she drove by me and didn't stop, I got into my car, a blue 61 Corvair, put on my trousers and followed this woman north for a distance, then stopped and repeated the same act I had done earlier. The woman didn't stop. I got into my car, followed her, passed her and did this act for the third time. The woman never stopped at any time until she pulled off the road at a service station in Jacksonville.

I drove on by her and I haven't seen her since.

I don't really know why I did this. I got a feeling that I wanted to expose myself to a woman, and the reason I was so persistent with this woman was because the more I did this, the better I felt, and I then thought I might get her to stop. If she had have stopped and been willing, I think I could have performed an act of sexual intercourse with her.

I get this urge to expose myself often, but I have enough willpower to restrain myself most of the time. It has been about a couple of weeks since I exposed myself. The last time was similar to what I did last night, except that I only stopped my car one time. This occurred between Beebe and Vilonia. I seldom do this, no more than once a month, and I usually masturbate after these acts. I have no desire for young girls and only want women, at least my age or older, when I expose myself.

During the last part of 1958, I tried to stop a woman in Beebe that I knew. I did the same thing with her that I did last night. She recognized me and notified James Welch, a deputy sheriff of Beebe and got together with my father and some more men in town and they all came to see me. During the conversation I agreed to see a psychiatrist and the matter at Beebe was kept pretty quiet. I didn't talk to the prosecuting attorney, and I was not charged with this crime.

I made one trip to Little Rock to see a psychiatrist and I don't recall his name. I don't really remember much about what he told me, but I do remember that he tried to point out to me the seriousness of what I had done. I know that it is serious, but when I get the urge to do this, I forget about the consequences.

This woman that recognized me at Beebe 5 years ago is Neona Heffner and she was in her 40s at that time. I had watched this woman for some time and thought about exposing myself to her for a long time before I actually got the nerve to do it. She was sexually attractive to me. She was a big built woman, but wasn't fat, brown hair, a little heavy in her legs and medium bust. I didn't know her personally and had never carried on a conversation with her. But the more I watched her, the more I wanted to expose myself to her and have sexual intercourse with her.

I knew about what time this woman closed her dress shop in Beebe and I knew where she lived about 5 or 6 miles out in the country from Beebe. On this evening that she recognized me, I had parked on the road to her house and when I saw her car coming, I stepped out of my car and stood beside the left side of my car as she drove by. I was naked from my waist down. This woman just drove by me and didn't slow down. About two days later, these people came to see me. That was the first time that I had ever performed this act, and after she drove on by, I think I masturbated before I got into my car and drove off. Since that time, and including last night, no woman has ever stopped when I would perform these acts. I date women occasionally and I have gone steady some, but I am not now. I had the urge while going steady, but I was always able to restrain from exposing myself during these times. One thing that might account for this is my occasional sexual intercourse with a steady girlfriend. As far as I know, these girlfriends knew nothing of my urge to expose myself. I last went steady in August of 1962.

I work for Westinghouse at Little Rock as a laborer, and I am now assigned to the first shift. I go to work at 7:00 a.m. and complete my normal shift at 3:30 p.m. I drive daily from Beebe to Little Rock and back to Beebe. I've worked this first shift from the last of August or 1st of September 1963. I recall the disappearance of Mrs. Stapleton at Searcy and remember that on the Friday before she disappeared, I burned 2 valves in my car. I worked on my car that weekend in the driveway of my yard, borrowed my mother's light green 56 Ford to drive to work Monday and Tuesday, then finished repairing my car late Tuesday night. The night she disappeared, I worked on this car until 10:30 or 11:00 p.m. I bought some parts at a little part store next door to my father's grocery store, most of them on Saturday October 5th, and I don't recall buying any parts after that.

There are two boys at Beebe that I run around with. One is Johnny Fisher, who is 23 years old and owns a 1963 maroon Chevrolet. He works for a contractor in and around Beebe. This man has never indicated to me that he has an abnormal sex drive. The other boy is Sheril Roush, 23 years old and he went into service on October 24th, 1963. He drives a red and white 1963 Ford. This man gives the appearance of having a normal sex drive.

I have furnished the above voluntary statement to investigator Bill Bogle and Sergeant W.A. Tudor at State Police Headquarters in Little Rock on November 10th, 1963, I have read this eight page handwritten statement, understand that it can be used in court both for or against me, and I find it true and correct.

Sammy S. Stanley

Grady Bankhead

❖❖

Supplement #47
This information was furnished by F.B.I. agents:

Grady A. Bankhead, 5158 Pineview Lane, formerly 114 Pineview Lane, was interviewed by Special Agents John C. McGinley and Frank A. Gilman at the mobile office of the F.B.I.

Bankhead was advised that he did not have to make a statement, that any statement he did make could be used in court against him, and that no threats or promises would be made to him to induce him to make this statement. He was further advised of his right to an attorney.

Bankhead stated that he first met Doctor E.R. Stapleton in Monroe, LA, while hitchhiking from Tucson, AZ to Mobile, AL. He stated it was late at night and Doctor Stapleton was driving a pickup truck. After picking him up on the highway, Doctor Stapleton invited him to spend the night at his residence.

At that time, Doctor Stapleton was teaching at Northeast Louisiana State College, Monroe, LA. After arriving at Doctor Stapleton's residence, Doctor Stapleton approached him and did commit an unnatural sex act against him. No one else was at Doctor Stapleton's residence at this time. Bank had remained overnight, and the next morning Doctor Stapleton took him back to the highway where he hitchhiked on to Mobile. He stated, as he recalled, this was early in 1959.

Approximately 3 weeks after arriving in Mobile, Bankhead stated he started receiving letters from Doctor Stapleton. These letters were very intimate. Subsequently, Dr. Stapleton advised him by letter that he had moved to Commerce, Texas, where he would teach at East

Texas State College and if, he, Bankhead would come to Commerce and live with him, he would help him enter college there as well as help him find a job. After several requests from Doctor Stapleton, he decided to go to Commerce, TX.

Upon his arrival there, he moved into the residence of Doctor Stapleton, which was located on Greenville St., about two blocks from the East Texas State College campus. He believes he arrived there sometime during the latter part of 1959. Subsequently, he enrolled in an advanced lineal type and printing course at this college and attended school about two months. He claimed to have enrolled under his true name at the beginning of school, but at the beginning of the second semester, he filled out enrollment papers using the name of his brother, James Clayton Bankhead, so that he could use his brother's GI Bill of Rights. Subsequently, he was asked for the discharge papers of his brother to verify that he had been in the military service and when he was unable to produce these papers, he was not allowed to enter the college.

Bankhead stated he lived with Doctor Stapleton about two months, and during this time Doctor Stapleton bought him cigarettes and gave him spending money. Also, during this time Doctor Stapleton committed a number of unnatural sex acts against him. He denied committing any unnatural sex acts against Doctor Stapleton, claiming that he himself was not a homosexual. During this period of time, Bankhead stated that due to Doctor Stapleton's homosexual activities, he attempted to leave two or three times. But that each time Doctor Stapleton would beg him to stay, cry, and he would then give in and stay on at Doctor Stapleton's residence. At no time while he was at Doctor Stapleton's residence did Doctor Stapleton bring any of his homosexual friends or associates to his home, and at no time did he ever meet any friends or associates of Doctor Stapleton, other than Doctor Stapleton's brother, mother, wife, and daughter, whose names he does not recall.

Bankhead stated Dr. Stapleton would be gone from the apartment two or three nights a week and he believed that Doctor Stapleton was driving the highways, picking up hitchhikers and committing unnatural sex acts against those he picked up, as this was apparently the way he made his contacts.

Bankhead advised that after not being allowed to enroll in school, he decided to leave Doctor Stapleton and return to Mobile. Doctor

Stapleton took him from Commerce to Dallas, TX, gave him $90, and that is the last time he saw Doctor Stapleton and he has not heard from him since that time.

At no time did he ever attempt to extort any money from Doctor Stapleton, and he knows no one who ever attempted to extort money from him, he stated. Further, he knows of no illegal activities in which Doctor Stapleton is involved other than being a homosexual.

Bankhead advised that Doctor Stapleton always spoke highly of his wife, stating only that they could not get along when living together. Mr. Stapleton claimed that his wife was not aware that he was a homosexual. Bank had further advised that Doctor Stapleton has never met his brother, Jake Clayton Bankhead, and only knows this name inasmuch as he attempted to enroll at East Texas State College under this name, he stated. In fact, neither he nor his mother knew the present whereabouts of his brother and neither of them have heard from him in about three years. Bankhead advised he has been in jail a few times, but only for being drunk and claims to have committed no other crimes.

He advised that in about 1948 or 1949, he was a member of the Texas Police Department and was married to Jane Anderson, whose present whereabouts he does not know, as they are divorced. Bankhead stated he has been working at summer resorts returning to Mobile about October 1st, 1963, and upon arriving in Mobile has not been out of town. He advised he definitely was not in or near Searcy, AR on October 8th, 1963, and was not aware that the wife of Doctor Stapleton had been murdered.

Bankhead advised that at no time did he ever meet any friends or associates of Dr. Stapleton, nor did Dr. Stapleton reveal the identities of any of his friends or associates, apparently keeping his associates separated.

Joesph Aloysius Worm Jr

❖❖

Supplement #63

I, Joseph Aloysius Worm, Jr., give the following voluntary statement to sergeant W.A. Tudor, at the State Police Headquarters in Little Rock, Arkansas on December 16, 1963.

One day last summer, about 12:30 p.m. I was driving from Morrilton to Little Rock in my 1963 Chevy Nova Sedan, color, saddle tan, when I noticed a man hitchhiking along Highway 64 near the freight depot just east of Morrilton. I picked up this man who told me his first name was Karl and I don't recall his last name. As I drove toward Little Rock, this man told me that he was going to meet a friend in Little Rock at the "Y" and further along in the conversation, he said that he had hitchhiked from Los Angeles California where he had recently stayed at the Hotel Cecil. I was familiar with it as I had stayed there while I was in the navy and once, summer before last, while I was visiting in California. This man mentioned that both he and his friend the one he was visiting in Little Rock, had stayed in this motel together. I stopped at my mother's house, on Route Two, Conway, where Karl and I both had lunch, and then we traveled to Little Rock. Karl had mentioned that he had no money and was down on his luck. I felt sorry for him and told him that he could stay with me at my apartment, 1515 West 8th street Apt #5 in Little Rock, until his friend arrived in Little Rock, which was to be the following Tuesday or Wednesday. The day of the week that I picked him up was Sunday.

We arrived at my apartment about 2:30 p.m. and Karl stayed at my apartment until the next morning, and I dropped him off at the Greyhound Bus Station in Little Rock as I went to work. I gave him a card with the Double R Florist's name and my name and phone number across the top. I told Karl to call me if his friend did not come in, and he didn't have a place to stay that night. I went on to work and after lunch Karl called me at work and told me that his friend was in town and that he wouldn't be at the apartment that night.

Karl called me about every day that week and about Wednesday of that week, he called me at work and asked me if he could spend the night at my apartment. I asked him first why he wasn't staying with his friend and professor from Harding College, and he said they were going to Florida for a few days. I told him that he could stay at my apartment. That night I picked him up from in front of the

Continental Bus Station in Little Rock as I came from work and took him to my apartment. Karl had been drinking, and when I asked him where he got the money to buy drinks, he said that his friend's professor friend had given his friend a hundred dollars before he left for Florida and that his friend had given him part of the money. I asked Karl where he had been staying, and he remarked that he was staying with his friend at the Capitol Hotel. During the course of the conversation Karl related that the Professor was planning to divorce his wife and move away with Karl's friend to live with him because of their intellectual interest. Karl didn't say much more about the professor except that the professor had been furnishing them money.

Karl stayed with me that night and the next morning I let him out of my car at Fifth and Main in Little Rock. The next day, on Friday, Karl called me at work and wanted to stay another night with me and asked me to pick him up. I told him that my cousin, Fred Worm, Jr. had called and asked me to supper, and I didn't know what his plans were. Karl asked me to meet him at the Gar Hole around nine and I told him that I couldn't promise that I would be there, because I didn't know my cousins' plans. He asked me if he could spend the night and I told him he could spend the night if he could be there no later than eleven.

About 1:30 a.m. Karl knocked on my door and I let him in. Karl was drunk and remonstrated with me for not meeting him at the Gar Hole, and then started telling me his past troubles and got on a "crying jag." Karl mentioned that he had been in a car wreck and that he was responsible for this accident, which killed the girl he loved. Karl got into such a state that I became concerned for my safety, and I slept very little that night.

That night I woke up thinking that I didn't want anybody like that around me. The next morning, I let Karl out of my car at Jacksonville, and he told me that he was hitchhiking to Nashville, Tennessee. The following week, about Monday or Tuesday, I saw Karl in the Gar Hole at the Marion Hotel, and he apologized for the way he had acted at my house the last night he stayed there and remarked that he had called a sister who was sending him money to travel home. He said that he was leaving the following day.

At no time did Karl propose a homosexual act to me, or me to him for that matter. I have never proposed a homosexual act to anyone.

I recall hearing on the radio or television about the disappearance of Mrs. Stapleton at Searcy and the next morning Mrs. Rainwater asked me if I had heard about it and made a casual remark about it being terrible. I know I worked the day before, but I can't tell you where I was that night. I know for sure that I don't know Mrs. Stapleton, had nothing to do with her death and I know nothing about her disappearance or death.

I have read the above six-page statement, initiated the corrections, find it true and correct to the best of my knowledge.

Joseph A. Worm, Jr.

Billy Joe Rust
◆◆

Supplement #49
Information Concerning the whereabouts of Billy Joe Rust /white male.

Information from the F.B.I. reveals that Billy Joe Rust, Texas department of Correction No. 167335, was committed to the Texas Prison, Sandy Point on May 3rd, 1962, and is currently serving his sentence there.

Melvin Lewis Jones
◆◆

Melvin Jones statement March 18th, 1969

Interview of Melvin Lewis Jones, W/M. D.O.B. 11-13-36. F.B.I. No. 701 186 B. Presently in custody, Wilburton, Oklahoma.

INFORMATION TO BE HELD AS CONFIDENTIAL:

On March 18th, 1969, Lieutenant Young received information that the above-named subject had some information in reference to a murder that occurred in White County of a schoolteacher and also information in reference to another murder that occurred at Bismarck, Arkansas of subject Ken Langston. (Note: Langston and Laxton are in the file presumably being the same person) Telephone check with Lieutenant W.A. Tudor revealed that the murder victim in White County was Frances Stapleton, that she was murdered in White County, that she had gone in a laundry in Searcy and her car later found still parked at the laundry early next a.m., this being October 8th, 1963, and that the body found the 19th of October, 1963 about 9 miles south of Searcy. No information and files reference Kent Langston.

On arrival in Wilburton, Kevin Melvin Jones was interviewed. The subject very hard to interview as he talks at random. However, he furnished the following information.

It is his belief that this subject, Nolan Hickman, did kill Mrs. Stapleton. Or if he did not, that he has personal knowledge of the crime, that the informant was raised in the Bradford, Denmark area and that he knows Nolan Hickman very well. That Hickman does a lot of drinking, and when the subject is drinking, he does a lot of talking. That Hickman has talked about the murder of Mrs. Stapleton and has described the murder in detail that the victim did have cotton stuffed in her mouth. He had previously stated to Oklahoma officer Crane that the victim also had cotton stuffed in the vagina and rectum. However, he did not state the latter information to this agent. Also, that the victim was mutilated.

Informant further advised that Everett Guthrie did kill a Mr. Western and did use the shotgun of Nolan Hickman. This occurred in Jackson County. That the subjects were tried and acquitted on this charge in Jackson County. Everett Guthrie is supposed to have called Mr. Weston to the front door of his home and shot him with a shotgun of Nolan Hickman. Western's son, Lewis (DUB) Western, has also served time in the Arkansas State PEN and has stated that he has been said to rough up some persons and on one occasion did use a knife on his subject in Blytheville.

Informant further advised that he had heard Nolan Hickman state that he was going to kill Kent Laxton, whose body was found in cemetery at Denmark. This person was shot in the head twice and also beaten. The body of Laxon was found in his truck by a brother, Sonny Laxton That this murder occurred after the murder of Mrs. Stapleton, that Nolan Hickman, Everett Guthrie, Kent Laxton, and Lewis Western are the persons that killed the teacher, that Laxton was getting nervous and was killed by Hickman because he was afraid that he would talk.

Informant further advised that at the time of the murder of the teacher that DOPE was very plentiful on the campus at Harding and that she was instrumental in putting a stop to the dope racket and that persons involved are the ones that killed her.

Informant further advised OHP Trooper Cranes that, Bobby Laxton was killed in a car accident between Bradford and Denmark, that Nolan Hickman had done something to Bobby Laxton's car and that Nolan Hickman stated that he got him and that if he was caught up with this, he could get out of it because he was Nolan Hickman. Also, that Nolan's son was with Bobby Laxton at the time that the accident occurred at the bottom of Glaze Creek Hill.

Further, that Nolan Hickman had cosigned the note with Bobby Laxton on the automobile. It is his belief that this may have had something to do with the murder of Kent Laxton also.

Informant further advise that there are other persons who will have about the same information as he has, and they are LeReace Throckmortin, who lives at Denmark, and DeReace Throckmortin, who lives at Bradford. Also, a Sheila Gay who lives at Bald Knob, and that if they have not been interviewed, they should be in connection with the murder of Mrs. Stapleton, and also Kent Laxton.

Informant advised that a person known to him as Clinton Kirk, who has served time for a sex offense, also may have some knowledge of the murder of Mrs. Stapleton and was sent up from White County, believed to be in 1964. He advised that Kirk may not know Hickman; he does not know for sure.

Informant further advised that at the time of the murder of Mrs. Stapleton that a student at Harding College known to him as a D.D. Rand and supposed to be from Denison, TX was supposed to have good contacts and could get anything done for a price.

Received March 20th, 1969.

Douglas Dwaine Martin

❖❖

Supplement #63

FULL STATEMENT

Douglas Dwaine Martin gave the following voluntary statement to Chief Deputy Sheriff Benson Robbins and State Police Sergent W.A. Tudor at the Sheriff's office in Searcy, Arkansas on December 31, 1963, at 11:45 a.m.

I am Douglas Dwaine Martin, white male, born at Wolfe Bayou in Cleburne County, Arkansas on May 25, 1936, and am the son of Jena Roseana Foshee and Henry Martin. My father is divorced from my mother and lives in Porterville, California. My parents have been divorced for twenty-six years and my mother is now married to Danny Foshee and he and my mother live on the V. J. Brady Place at Route 3, Vilonia, Arkansas.

I am 5'8 tall, weigh about 140 pounds, brown hair and blue eyes and I have a long horizontal scar along my left side that was caused by removing a lung.

I was reared in the area of Enola, Arkansas and went to school at Enola, finishing the tenth grade. I was taking the 11th and 12th together when I quit school in about 1955. I had quit in 1954 and went to Little Rock, where I worked at Fones Brothers Hardware for about two months, and I then enlisted in the Air Force. I was in the Air Force for four months and received a general discharge under honorable conditions I was stationed at Lackland Air Force Base in San Antonio, TX when I was working as Barracks guard at a time when some of the men began to rough up the barracks. I knew that if I didn't report it and it was observed by my superiors that I would be in trouble and I knew that if I did report it, I would be in trouble. I decided to report the matter. That night I was thrown out of a second-floor window of the barracks and the other men in the barracks told that I jumped out. The Air Force put me in the hospital for about a month or better and discharged me because of my supposed nervous condition. After my discharge, I came home to Plumerville where my folks were then farming. I forgot to mention that I had gone to school at Plumerville for about a year before I quit and went into the Air Force.

After returning to Plumerville, I worked for a few weeks at Elmer's Firestone at Conway. I quit that job and married Bobby Lou McCoy of Plumerville, a girl that I had known about a month. I was married to her for about 6 weeks when we got into an argument. Just over nothing. I told her that I was going hunting and went into the bedroom and got my shotgun. When I came out of the bedroom, I told her that I was going hunting, and I had the shotgun in one hand and two or three shells in my pocket. She said something about having heard about people going hunting and then shooting their wife. I told her something like I didn't think she was worth shooting. About that time, my brother, Palmer Lee Bates, his wife, and I think that my mother and step daddy came in and my brother took my wife to her folks. I just walked away from the house to settle down my nerves. I was gone about a couple of hours and returned to the house. My folks were still there. We were living in the house with them at the time. My wife didn't come back to live with me and about a week later I went into a cafe at Morrilton to eat dinner and I saw my wife there. I tried to talk to her, and she got mad. She told me that she was going to call the police and I told her that I would do it for her. I called the police, and they came to Warrens Cafe, picked me up and put me in jail. I think the sheriff took me to the state hospital that same afternoon.

I stayed in the state hospital in Little Rock for about 30 days starting in July 1955 and I was given yard privilege. One afternoon, just before they closed the doors, I walked away from the state hospital without authorization and went to Joe Gilley's farm on U.S. 64 east of Conway and spent the night in his barn. I picked cotton the next day for Check Harris and went on to my stepfather's house at Menifee that evening.

I had been at my stepfather's house for three or four days, maybe a week, when the Sheriff from Morrilton came out to the house and he and the highway patrolman who came out there with the sheriff talking for a few minutes and the patrolman told the sheriff that I didn't look crazy to him, and he walked off. The sheriff followed him, and they both left me at my stepfather's house, where I stayed until about November 1955. About that time, I hitchhiked to San Diego, CA where I was arrested for investigation of desertion. They fingerprinted me, kept me 4 days and turned me loose. I left San Diego. When they turned me out of jail, and I hitchhiked back home I was gone from home about two or three weeks during this trip.

I think that winter is the time my stepfather moved back to the Enola area and as best I remember, I went back to school at Enola. That year I was taking the 11th and 12th grades together under the GI Bill when I quit after going about six months.

After I quit school, I think that I then hitchhiked to Louisiana, going nowhere in particular with more or less just to get away from Enola and look for something else to do. I had hitchhiked to Monroe, LA, and was hitchhiking, going towards Shreveport, when a man driving a 56 Chevrolet pickup, stopped and picked me up. He just asked the general questions about how I was, where I was going, talked about the weather and just regular conversation. He asked me where I was from, who I was and what I was doing in Louisiana when I told the man that I was from near Vilonia, AR, the man told me that he was Doc Stapleton from the College at Monroe and that he was from Searcy and had taught at Harding College there. He then began to ask me about how I would like to go to college and questions that made me think that he wanted to help me for some reason or other. He picked me up right after dinner and Doc Stapleton asked me if I was hungry. And I told him that I wasn't. He then took me to get a malt, and while we were having this malt, the doc asked me if I wanted to go up to his house with him and rest a couple of days and look for a job. I agreed to stay at his house and Doc told me that he would help me find a job there in Monroe. I went to his house located on a main highway just outside of Monroe about 5 miles east. It was a big white colonial type house that was 100 years old.

About 7:00 or 8:00 that night, the doc wanted to give me a bath, and I didn't want any part of that bath. The doc rubbed his hands over my body some and handled my privates and then I agreed to take a bath. I took a bath, and the doc dried me off with a towel. The doc wanted to go to bed, and we did. Both of us stripped off naked and the doc loved around on me just like you would a woman for a little while and the doc then went down on me and sucked my dick After that we both went to sleep.

This act was repeated time and time again while I stayed there for a few weeks. I became disgusted with what I was doing, and the more I thought about what Doc was doing and the kids he was teaching at the college, the more I wanted to do something about it. I was working at the Twin City Glass Company in Monroe, and I told the foreman there how I was living and what the doc was doing. This foreman suggested that I go to the police with it and this gave me enough courage to do just that. The doc had several pictures drawn of male sex organs at the house, and the police went with me to pick up Doc and went with both of us out to Doc's house. The police saw these drawn pictures and I believe that Doc was arrested. I knew that the police told me to get out of town and I left my job. At no time did I tell the doc that if he didn't buy me an automobile that I was going to tell on him.

I had been staying with the doc at his house in Monroe about two or three weeks when he decided to come to Searcy, and I came with him. We drove to the doc's house first. It seems like it was late in the evening. I know that his boy and girl was at home, and I remember that his wife was there. I stayed at the house about 15 minutes and then I took the doc's truck and drove to Enola to visit my folks. I spent the night with them, and the next morning I drove the doc's truck back to Searcy and went to Doc's house and I think I went into the living room for a few minutes and saw that Doc, his wife, and his children were there. We stayed a few minutes and then started driving toward Louisiana.

Another incident that occurred while I was living with Doc Stapleton in Monroe was when his wife and children came to see him. I don't know whether it was before or after he made the trip to Searcy, but it was seems like it was a week after that when Mrs. Stapleton and her two children drove her car to Monroe and spent overnight with Doc. Mrs. Stapleton left the next morning with the kids and I haven't seen her since that time.

I remember this about the Stapleton house, which I have only been inside on 2 occasions for a very short time. It faces towards the college, has a garage on the west side, a driveway leading to the garage, has carpet on the living room floors, on the east side of the room a couch was against the wall, against the north wall of this room was an easy chair, a television set was against the south wall, and it seems like I can remember a tall old type piano in the living room along the west wall.

After this incident with the police at Monroe, LA, I think that I hitchhiked home to Enola. I don't exactly recall when it was, but about that time I went back to California and worked for the Golden Eagle service station, 150 S. Sepulveda at either La Segundo or Culver City, CA. I worked there for about four months. I had hitchhiked to California with Juanita Lacey, 1301 S El Dorado AR. I had met this girl while I was in the state hospital at Little Rock and had spent several weeks with her and her folks at El Dorado before we started hitchhiking to California. After we got to California, her father came to California and picked the girl up and I stayed out there for a while and worked at the service station. I hitchhiked back home and stayed around Enola working around there on the farm for most of the year 1958 and part of 1959, except for the time that I went to Florida I worked for John's Flower Nursery, Apopka, Florida during the winter and I think that it was 1958.

I know that I was home during the summer of 1959 and on September 5th, 1959, I married Margaret Bacus who was living at Conway at the time. We have three children. The oldest is Carol Janice, born July 5th, 1959, and this is not my child, the middle-aged child is Jenny Lee, born May 17th, 1961, and the youngest is Douglas Dwayne Junior, born May 18th, 1962.

After I got married, we lived on the farm for about a month and we'd moved to Little Rock, where we lived at several addresses while I worked for the Colony Furniture Company of Little Rock. I quit my job there in 1960, May, and we left Little Rock and went to Vancouver, WA to see my brother Lloyd Martin, who I hadn't seen since I was a little boy. I stayed there for about two months and worked at a box spring factory. Then my family and I left there and moved to a little town about 30 miles this side of Portland, where we stayed for about a month. We came back to Arkansas and back to the farm at Enola. I worked on the farm until this past May, at which time I went to work for Jim Fecher at Fecher's DX station. At that time, I was driving a two tone 1955 Pontiac that I had bought from Pruitt's Motor Company in Conway. I traded this car for a 1949 International truck while I was working for Fecher and made this trade with Pipkin at Ward, AR. I traded this truck for a 1953 Ford at the D&M garage at Beebe and I was driving this car when I went to work for John Hawes at the Hawes mobile station at Beebe House. This was about September 1963. I let this car go back to D&M garage and then I bought a 1955 Pontiac Color light green over dark green at Pruitt Motor Company and Conway. I still own this car and it is stored in the yard of the place I lived in Beebe. I threw 2 rods in this car, and I can't drive it. It was about the second week in November when I threw those rods out.

During the first week of November, I went to work for Mr. Carl Rogers at the Bel-Mar Esso station in Beebe, and I am working there now.

On October 8, 1963, I was working for John Hawes at his service station, was driving this two-tone green 1955 Pontiac, and living with my wife and children right down from the hill from Wheelers Dairy. My house was about two miles off Highway 64 north on a dirt road that interacts with U.S 64 at Barrentine's Store. I don't recall but I may have been driving that white over maroon 1953 Ford that I let go back to D&M's garage on the day of Mrs. Stapleton's disappearance.

As best I can remember, I worked on Tuesday, October 8th, 1963, until about 6 p.m. It was Johnny's Lightfoot's day off, but what I did after I got off work is what I can't remember. I normally go right home, and my family and I could have gone to Des Arc to visit my wife's folks, or we could have gone to Vilonia, visiting my folks, or we may have gone to Conway to visit my wife's sister. We make these trips occasionally on the evening before my day off the following day. I know that I was off duty on Wednesday, October 9th.

I am willing to submit a polygraph examination concerning my activities on that day.

I want to mention that I have seen Doc Stapleton once since I reported him to the police in Monroe, LA. About two years after that incident in Louisiana, I was at home on the farm at Enola, AR, with my stepfather and mother and two other men that were chopping cotton for us when Doc Stapleton drove up to the house in a Cadillac automobile that he told us he had just bought. He said that he just wanted to come and see me to see how I was doing, and he wanted to know if I wanted to go riding with him. I told him no. He stayed at the house about an hour or so and he left. He was friendly and didn't seem mad about what had happened in Monroe.

The only other homosexual that I have had contact with was also in Monroe, LA. This man's name is Frank Brinnon, and he operated a furniture store in Monroe. I was in Monroe to see a girlfriend about two years before I met Stapleton and got a job at this furniture store on February 12th, 1955. On the second or third day of March, I quit because Brinnon was a cock sucker. He would pay me $20 to let him suck my dick. I didn't give a shit then and I needed the money, but I got tired of this and quit my job. I have read the above 4-page typewritten statement initialed the corrections, find it true and correct to the best of my knowledge.

Douglas Martin - Witness Vincent Robbins.

DAVID SMART REPORT

◈

Sergeant R.E. Hancock, Criminal Investigation Division, Alabama State Police Post Office Drawer See Decatur, AL 35601, telephoned today to report the following information. The skeletal remains of David Smart, an aerospace engineer for NASA at Decatur, AL, was found in a wooded area near Decatur on August 13th, 1974. Smart died from a gunshot wound between his eyes and no weapon was found in the area of the skeleton. Smart attended college at Harding in Searcy during early 1963 and was said to have been involved in homosexual acts with other students and employees of the college, including a Dr. Stapleton, whose wife was murdered in Searcy during 1963. Smart was reported to have associated with homosexuals and was occupying a $75 per month apartment which is described as nothing more than a dump, although he enjoyed a $17,000 per year salary. Sergeant Hancock asks that we conduct an investigation at the College in Searcy to determine all information available to them concerning Smarts attendance there. His associates, his conduct, any record of his employers and places of residence. Inquiry, then, should be made of those employers, associates, landlords, and neighbors to determine if he may have been involved in homosexual activity and for the identity of persons he may have contacted after leaving the college and Searcy. Please route me the file on the murder of Mrs. Stapleton and I'll pursue it for any information that may be of help to Sergeant Hancock. From Major W.A. Tutor, September 12th, 1974.

POLYGRAPHS

❖

Polygraphs, also known as lie detectors, can be a useful tool in certain contexts such as law enforcement investigations, pre-employment screenings, and security clearance assignments. They are designed to measure physiological responses such as heart rate, blood pressure, and skin conductivity, which can indicate signs of stress or deception. While not admissible as evidence in all courts, polygraphs can sometimes provide valuable leads or corroborate other evidence in investigations. Additionally, the mere presence of a polygraph examination can deter individuals from providing false information, making it a useful tool for screening purposes. However, it's important to note polygraphs are not foolproof and can be influenced by various factors, including the individual's physiological makeup and the skill of the examiner.

A couple of things to note. Ray Stapleton stated he would take a polygraph and later changed his mind and did not go through with the exam. As always in cases as cold as this one, there are missing files, so if Ray changed his mind yet again, and took a test, it could be missing. There is a strong likelihood of other polygraph reports being missing as well because there are only a few in the files I could find. I have included as much information as I could decipher that I received from my FOIA request.

I noticed on Glen Dewey and Mary Claire's results, for the question of whether they knew who killed their mother, they each answered no but their response of "no" was marked guilty by the examiner. At the bottom of Mary Claire's polygraph report was the statement hers was a guilty response due to the thought her brother was guilty.

In 1993, my mother had a conversation with Mary Claire, and at that time she stated she did not think her brother was guilty in any way. There could be a myriad of reasons as to why both responses showed up as guilty. In 1963, Mary Claire was traumatized, grieving, shocked, and at the mercy of the information her father Ray was feeding her. Ray was saying things behind closed doors to the effect, "Now that your mother is gone, we can do more things. You can start piano lessons again." Ruby was frugal and that could possibly be the reason she stopped Mary Claire's piano lessons. We know from Clarita's statement Ray was also telling Mary Claire things about his separation from her mother that painted Ruby in a bad light.

Glen Dewey learned of his father's secrets and undoubtedly would consider all possibilities relating to Ray's acquaintances. That was easy to glean. Each went on to explain their thoughts, confirming they did, at least in that moment, have a suspect in mind. One more reason to crack open this case and take a deeper look.

Before each polygraph the description below was given. I am only including it once and then will list all responses below.

The subject willingly submitted to the examination and was examined in a private room. The Polygraph Test itself consisted of the following: blood pressure cuff was placed about the upper arm directly over the Brachial Artery and inflated to a point about midway between the systolic and diastolic pressures, so that a continuous tracing of the blood pressure-pulse variations were recorded by a stylus on a moving strip of paper. A tube (Pneumograph) was fastened about the chest for transmitting respiratory changes to the instrument. An electrode was placed in contact with the palm of the hand for recording electrodermal responses. A normal reading was first obtained, then two irrelevant questions were asked, and finally relevant questions pertaining to the case in question were interspersed with the irrelevant questions and the subject was instructed to answer all the questions with "Yes" or "No".

Glen Dewey Stapleton

Question 1
Do you know who killed your mother?
"No"
Guilty Reaction

Question 2
Did you kill your mother?
"No"
No guilty reaction

Question 3
Did you harm your mother the night of her disappearance?
"No"
No guilty reaction

Question 4
Did you lie on this test?
"No"
Guilty reaction

Subject does not know who killed his mother. Suspects one of his father's homosexual friends. Subject did not kill his mother. Subject did not harm his mother. Subject reacted to question 3 and 9 however reacting to thoughts and not guilt.

Mary Claire Stapleton

Question 1
Do you know who killed your mother?
"No"
Guilty reaction

Question 2

Did you kill your mother?
"No"
No guilty reaction

Question 3
Did you employ someone to kill your mother?
"No"
No guilty reaction

Question 4
Have you lied on this test?
"No"
Guilty reaction

Subject thinks brother Glen Dewey killed mother, subject did not kill her mother, subject did not employ anyone to kill her mother, subject did lie on the test on question 1.

Douglas Dwaine Martin

Question 1
Did you know Mrs. Stapleton?
"Yes"
No guilty reaction

Question 2
Have you seen Mrs. Stapleton in the past year?
"No"
Guilty reaction

Question 3
Did you talk to Mrs. Stapleton in Washeteria the day of her disappearance?
"No"
No guilty reaction

Question 4
Were you involved with a homosexual?
"No"
Guilty reaction

Question 5
Have you lied on this test?
"No"
Guilty reaction

Subject did know Mrs. Stapleton, has seen Mrs. Stapleton in the past year, did not talk to Mrs. Stapleton the day she vanished, has been involved with a homosexual, subject lied on test, questions 4 and 5.

Samuel Sterling Stanley

Question 1
Did you know Mrs. Stapleton?
"No"
No guilty reaction

Question 2
Did you talk to Mrs. Stapleton the day of her disappearance?
"No"
No guilty reaction

Question 3
Have you ever been involved with a sex-crime?
"Yes"
Guilty reaction, with admission

Question 4
Have you lied on this test?
"No"
No guilty reaction

Subject did not know Mrs. Stapleton, did not talk to Mrs. Stapleton the day of her disappearance, did not leave washeteria with Mrs. Stapleton, has been involved in a previous sex-crime, has not lied on this test.

James Brown Junior

Question 1
Have you told all the places you broke into?
"Yes"
Guilty reaction

Question 2
Have you ever broken into any place in Searcy?
"No"
Guilty reaction

Question 3
Do you know who killed Mrs. Stapleton?
"No"
No guilty reaction

Question 4
Have you lied on this test
"No"
Guilty reaction

Subject has not told all the places he burglarized, he has burglarized places in Searcy, he does not know who killed Mrs. Stapleton, he has lied on this test, 1,2 and 4. Subject is extremely nervous, heart rate is extremely rapid, respiration rate is high, however responses are what would be expected.

DESCRIPTION OF CLOTHING

❖❖

Supplement #15

A description of the clothing worn and the articles in possession of the victim on the night of her disappearance are enclosed as Supplement #15 with this report.

The victim's two children and her niece, Clarita Bartley, describe the victim's dress as follows.

Made of thin cotton material, white background and irregular shaped black figures which form an irregular checked design. This dress was fitted with a straight skirt and belt of matching material.

She was wearing shoes described as black flats pointed toe and worn in appearance, described as about size 6.

Her underclothing consisted of full slip, bra, panty girdle and brief type panty.

She wore no jewelry except possible plain black earrings and was carrying a black plastic purse finished to look like very soft grain leather, purse about 12 inches long, 5 inches in height is a clutch type with silver finish snap at the top center and silver finish band extending across the top of the purse and down each side to the hinge.

AUTOPSY

❖

Supplement #1
10-26-63

Mrs. E.R. Stapleton: 57, White, Female

Final Pathology
1. *Badly decomposed human body*
2. *Broken hyoid bone*
3. *Broken thyroid cartilage*
4. *Cotton bolos in mouth area*

The autopsy of this badly decomposed human body showed in addition to several soft tissue destruction, a broken hyoid bone and broken thyroid cartilage. Also, a large cotton bolus was found in the mouth area.

This badly decomposed human body was found in a creek bed near Beebe AR at 5:00 p.m. on 10/19/63. The body was referred to the University of Arkansas Medical Center for aid in identification. At the time the body was found, it was allegedly nude with no pieces of clothing, rings, watches, etc. found on or near the body. Autopsy was prepared by Alan Foster, corner of White County, Arkansas.

This is the moderately severe decomposed remains of a female. Although it is impossible to state exactly at this time whether the body was white or colored, it looks as if it was white. The skin and soft tissues about the head, face and neck have largely been lost with bone showing at numerous places. Most of the hair has been lost from the scalp and the scalp is partly missing. The skin over the remainder of the body is partially mummified and discolored.

Upon receipt of the body, the skull is found to be sitting on the thorax at an odd angle and the right arm is bent at 90° under the back the fingers pressing on the left side. The breasts are that of a female, apparently. Three or four long abrasions are noted on the abdomen starting in the area of the genitalia and running upward to the area of the left breast. These are noted to fan out in a sweeping fashion over the left upper chest and breast area. As previously noted, most of the soft tissues about the head is missing. The mandible is largely free.

The following is a summation of the dental characteristics of this body.
1) Upper left ridge: first molar missing. A second molar filled. Third molar filled.
2) Left Lower ridge: Left molar missing second molar filled. Third molar filled.
3) Upper right ridge: 2nd Premolar Missing. 1st molar filled, second molar filled, 3rd molar missing.
4) Lower right ridge: first premolar filled, last molar apparently missing, although this is difficult to determine exactly. The remaining 2 molars are filled. The left upper central incisor has been capped completely with a characteristic appearance on X-ray examination. This tooth is saved to compare with dental files which have been received from the dental files of Frances Ruby Stapleton of Searcy, AR

Upon examining the mouth cavity, a large cotton bolus the size of a clenched fist is noted in the mouth and upper throat region. This will be saved for possible toxicology determination.

Thoracic Cavity and Pleural: The thoracic cavity opened in a straight mid line incision. Most of the soft tissues in thoracic cavity have been destroyed. There are no body fluids or anything resembling blood in the thoracic cavity.

Cartilage and Neck Structure: Upon examination the neck hyoid bone is noted to be broken at the mid position with the left cornua missing (that is to say the left cornua cannot be found in the necrotic tissue) Upon examining the larynx, the thyroid cartilage be noted to be torn or separated in midline with the softening in the upper anterior position. No other positive findings noted in the remaining in the trachea and mediastinal structures.

Abdominal Cavities: The sideline incision previously noted is extended downward to open the abdomen. The organs have largely been lost, but what portions of the abdominal viscera remain are in their apparent correct anatomical positions. The loop of the large bowl is noted adherent to the lower anterior abdominal wall, but no evidence of a surgical incision is noted in the overlaying skin.

Heart and Major Blood Vessels: Is noted, the tissue has largely been lost no irregularities are noted.

Lungs, Liver, GI Tract, Spleen, Pancreas, Kidneys, Adrenals: No irregularities can be demonstrated other than extensive tissue deconstruction.

Internal and external genitalia: This is apparently the external genitalia of a female, although there has been much tissue destruction here. The previously mentioned abrasions extend apparently down to the genitals. The internal genitalia are that of a female.

It is impossible to evaluate at this time what size this body was in life because of the extensive loss of subcutaneous fat and tissue. However, no scars, tattoos or other identifying marks are noted over the portion of skin that remains.

Brain and Pituitary: The brain and pituitary show no irregularities other than extensive tissue damage and necrosis. The brain has been reduced to a small solid mass of black necrotic tissue. No fractures can be seen in examining the cavities and skull.

X-ray of the skull, thoracic, and abdomen have been outlined and reveal no metallic foreign objects. Dental X-rays from that of Frances Ruby Lowry Stapleton have been obtained from a Searcy dentist and will be compared with the fillings shown in the skull film.

Fly larvae varying up to 2 inches were sent to the entomology department at the university of Arkansas Fayetteville AR for possible determination of the age of the larvae.

Statement received about
blood found on belt

November 13th, 1963
Sheriff's Office, Searcy, White County, Arkansas

This specimen consists of a 5" segment of a lady's belt includes the buckle. The buckle and outer surface of the belt are covered with a black and white fabric. Several brown stains are present. Testing of the stains by benzidine reaction are positive for blood. Extraction with saline and precipitin reaction with anti-human precipitin are positive. This indicates that the stains are human blood.

Dr. Hoke, M.D.
Deputy State Medical Examiner

Document of belt sent for
examination

1963, Doctor Tom D. Norman, State Medical Examiner at University of Arkansas Medical Center in Little Rock, AR. Attention Doctor Roy Hoke, Deputy Medical Examiner.

Dear Doctor Hoke, enclosed is a copy of our Crime Lab worksheet as per our conversation last week. You will note that this report indicates the belt was delivered to you and received from you. And we would appreciate the report on your findings at your convenience. Thank you for your cooperation and assistance in this matter. Yours very truly.

Paul R MacDonald, Captain, Commanding Criminal Investigation Division, Arkansas State Police, W.A. Tudor.

Overview of the Location of the Abduction and Recovery of the Body

❖

October 28, 1963

INVESTIGATORS: Benson Robbins Chief Deputy Sheriff of White County, Searcy Arkansas
W.A. Tudor, Sergeant, Criminal Investigation Division, Arkansas State Police

COUNTY: White

LOCATION: ABDUCTION- From a building housing the Norge Launderama, located adjacent to and connecting with the north wall of Harrison's Grocery, and situated 72 feet north of the intersection US 67 and state 267, 72 feet west of the paved area of US 67, outside and near the city limits of Searcy, AR. Death's exact location not determined at this writing. Body recovered in a creek bed of bull Bayou 36 feet west of a dim road, 389 feet South of the old McCrae Beebe Rd. half mile West of US 67, 1.3 miles north of the intersection north Beebe City route and US 67.

DATE AND TIME: ABDUCTION: October 8th, 1963, 10:10 p.m.-10:55 p.m.
DEATH: Not determined at this writing.

BODY RECOVERED: October 19th, 1963, 5:15 p.m.

VICTIM: Frances Ruby Lowery Stapleton White Female Date of

birth 2/27/04 9:10 E Center St. Searcy, AR.

CAUSE OF DEATH: Strangulation and or suffocation.

NAME OF PHYSICIAN: Doctor T.D. Norman, State Medical Examiner.
AUTOPSY REPORT: Enclosed as Supplement #1

PHOTOGRAPHERS: Paul Schalchlin, Trooper Identification Division, Arkansas State Police. Gene Kaufman, Sergeant Photographic Laboratory, Arkansas State Police.

MORTICIAN: Gail Williams, Daniel Funeral Home, Searcy AR

EVIDENCE AT SCENE: ABDUCTION: At 12:05 a.m. October 9th, 1963, investigators found the victims vehicle parked on the blacktop parking apron of the laundromat and headed toward the front wall of the structure at a point south of the front entrance door. A distance of about four feet separated the front bumper of the vehicle from the front wall of the structure.

Dryer #2 contained a quantity of damp clothing and the operating mechanism had not been started. Dryer #4 contained a quantity of damp clothing, the door to the dryer was open, and a dime was found in the coin slot of this dryer. However, the operating mechanism of the dryer had not been started. A clothes basket was on the floor in front of and between these two dryers.

A search of the victim's automobile revealed a dishpan identified as her property, located in the rear seat of the station wagon, and this pan contained a container of "Wisk" only partially full.

A search of the victim's automobile and the entire area of abduction failed to locate her purse or the keys to her automobile.

LOCATION OF BODY: At 5:15 p.m. October 19th, 1963, a witness found the victim's body lying in the soft dirt of a dry creek bed at the bottom of a soft dirt bank that measures 13 feet in height. The top of this bank is on a level plane and 22 feet west of a dim dirt road that parallels and follows Bull Bayou. This creek bank is covered with vegetation and fallen leaves.

A piece of driftwood, of an undetermined length, and a diameter of 1 ½ inches at a point where it intersects a direct line from the body to the top of the bank, is located on this creek bank and situated in an area about half the distance from the brink to the body and parallels the creek bed. This piece of driftwood is broken in the area where it intersects the direct line from the bank to the body, and the broken piece remains attached to the rest of the driftwood and points in the direction of the body.

A measured distance of 389 feet extends north between the area of the dim road, immediately adjacent to the spot where the body was found, and the old McRae Beebe Rd.

The victim's body was found lying on her back, headed toward the creek bank and her feet toward the creek bed. The left leg was outstretched, the right leg was bent at the knee, outward, until the bottom of the right foot was parallel with the left knee. The head was turned to the left until the left side of the face rested on the ground. The left arm was extended until the upper area was in line with the shoulder and the forearm was bent at the elbow at an angle near 90 degrees. The back of the entire left arm and left hand rested on the ground, and the fingers of this hand are loosely clenched. The right arm was bent at the elbow in an angle permitting the right hand to be concealed under the right side of the back at the waist.

A shallow cut extends from the area of the vagina up the front center of the torso to a point 5 inches below the throat. Another shallow cut angles up the chest and across the upper area of the left breast to the left collarbone. Three additional shallow cuts angle from the center of the torso at the midriff, up across the left chest and upper area of the left breast.

A search of the immediate area revealed a button located on the creekbank in an area immediately above the body and below the brink of this bank. A section of belt, containing the buckle, and measuring about 6 inches in length, was located in the creek bed at the bottom of the bank and immediately adjacent to the body.

Microscopic examination of this section of belt reveals that the belt was severed by a sharp instrument.

One half of a brassiere, severed in the area between the cups, was located under the victim's body.

The belt and button have been identified by the victim's daughter as being attached to the dress worn by the victim on the night of her disappearance.

A few minutes before 10 p.m. October 1963, October 8th, 1963, the victim arrived at the Norge Launderama in her white 1961 Comet Station Wagon and parked the vehicle in front parking area. The victim entered the structure and placed her soiled clothing contained in baskets on the floor. She engaged the attendant Mrs. CR Reggie, in brief conversation, then walked next door to Harrison's Grocery where she purchased a container of "Wisk" and promptly returned to the Launderama. The victim then began to wash her clothing and was so engaged when the attendant and her husband, an employee of Harrison's Grocery, closed the grocery and left the victim in the Launderama alone at 10:10 p.m.

James William, operator of the Searcy Roller rink, closed his business at 10:00 p.m. October 8th, 1963, and left the rink about 10:30 p.m. He drove the three miles distance to the area of abduction and as he passed the Norge Launderama between 10:30 and 10:40 p.m. he observed an unidentified woman alone in the Launderama apparently engaged in washing clothing.

Jack Gardner, employee of Porter Rodgers Farms, had washed his clothing earlier in the day of October 8th and left the clothing at the laundromat. At 10:55 p.m. on the same date, Gardner returned to the laundromat to pick up his clothing. He observed a white comet station wagon parked in front of the building and noticed a basket of clothing which appeared to have been a completed wash on the floor of the Launderama and in front of a dryer. He also noticed that the door of this dryer was open, and it was partially filled with clothing.

He observed no person in or around the Launderama.

At 12:00 midnight, October 8th, 1963, the Searcy Police Department received a complaint by phone from a female caller, who identified herself as Mary Claire Stapleton, had informed the police that her mother, Mrs. Ruby Stapleton had gone to the Norge Launderama to do her wash and had not returned. The caller requested that the police attempt to locate her mother and advise the caller of their findings.

Within minutes after the complaint was received, Officers Dean Hunter and Adam Woodruff traveled to the Norge Launderama and found evidence described above under the heading, Evidence at Scene: Abduction. These officers then contacted Mary Claire Stapleton at her residence by telephone and told her of their findings. Miss Stapleton asked these officers to call for her at her home and take her to the Laundromat.

The officers complied with this request, and after transporting Mary Claire Stapleton to the laundromat, they then drove her to the residence of her brother, Glen Dewey Stapleton, located on US 67 Route South of the laundromat. The officers and Miss Stapleton attempted to arouse Glen Dewey and his family, and after a few minutes, Glen Dewey came to the door in what was apparently a drowsy condition. The officers left Miss Stapleton at her brother's residence.

This Searcy Police Department then notified Sheriff Jack Price of this incident and a search of the area was started. Officer Adam Woodruff began a search along US 67. City route north of the abduction scene, and inspected the area around a service station, located immediately north of the abduction scene along the west side of the highway and found nothing unusual and the doors locked. He then proceeded to the next business establishment the City Tire Shop, located on the West side of US 67 and about one block north of the Norge Launderama. A search around this establishment revealed nothing to arouse his suspicion, and he observed no damage to the structure. Officer Woodruff estimates the time of this inspection at 12:45 a.m.

He continued a search of the area north of the abduction scene along the West side of the highway until he reached the Brookshire tire Shop located about two blocks north of the scene of abduction about 1:00 a.m. and observed that a glass pane had been broken from the overhead type garage door located in the north wall of the structure. Burglars had reached through this opening and unlocked the locking mechanism on this door and raised some to gain entry to the structure. Burglars had then closed the overhead door to a point about 1 foot above its normal closing position and had exited through the front door. After ransacking the structure and taking about $3 in change from the cash register, these burglars took no merchandise from a large quantity stored inside this structure. The area of entry and exit is not within sight of the Norge Launderama.

Later in the early morning of October 9th, about 2:00 a.m., Officer Woodruff again made an inspection of the City Tire Shop and at that time observed that the plate glass door used as a front entrance to this establishment had been broken out and glass was scattered throughout the interior of the office area and front surface area. Officer Woodruff stepped through the opening in this plate glass door shop and determined that burglars had ransacked the City Tire Shop and carried a small office cabinet into a rear room and forced open the locked door. Files in this cabinet were ransacked, but nothing was taken. Burglars then traveled throughout the tire shop and eventually took about $3 in change. Exit was apparently through the same door as entry. The point of entry into the City Tire Shop is blocked from direct view of the Norge Launderama by the South wall of the establishment.

THE END

~ ACKNOWLEDGEMENTS ~

I would like to thank all individuals who contributed their time and expertise to help bring this project to fruition. So many of you and you are so appreciated.

I would like to thank Clarita Bartley for her time and memories shared with me. Her willingness to share something so personal and close to her heart was invaluable in this book. Her firsthand knowledge truly made a difference in the overall vibration of my project. I thank her from the bottom of my heart.

I would like to thank Hannah Wood for the time spent on helping me with my research and the endless emails she endured from me. She contributed above and beyond in her actions and energy. She was a valuable part of this project.

Thank you to Jerry Bass. He was a delight to meet and very valuable in my research and journey.

Thank you to the brave woman who wanted to remain anonymous but was willing to share her story with me about her experience of being a young girl at Ruby's house when the belt and button were shown to Mary Claire. It provided such uniqueness to this story and a deeper understanding of how the tragic event affected people. I appreciate you.

Thank you to all the unnamed detectives and law enforcement that gave me insight to this case, whether it was your opinion or fact, your feedback has been invaluable.

I want to say thank you to the strangers I reached out to over the internet that took my call. They didn't just take my call; they became confidants and important sources for this story to be told.

To "Matilda's" daughter,

Your willingness to talk with me brought unforeseen blessings in my life and I am so thankful for you and for Shelbey.

Melinda, thank you for responding to my messages and talking with me about this case. I enjoyed your thoughts and speculations. I enjoyed our discussions and was glad I could pass an item along to you that was your late mother's.

Heather with the fresh hair, thank you for everything. Your listening ears, wisdom, and your support throughout these past couple of years have been invaluable.

Finally, I extend my appreciation to all my friends who have patiently been waiting for me to complete this book and patiently listened while I talked their ear off about it all the time. You are the best!

~ To My Family ~

To my husband Clark,
Thank you for believing in me even when I doubted myself. Thank you for giving me the time and space to complete this project. Thank you for supporting me on this project that has been ten years in the making. You never wavered in your interest or support, and I am grateful. Here's to more chapters together. I love you.

To my remarkable older son Samuel,
From the first moment I held you until now, your presence in my life has given me meaning and I am endlessly thankful for the lessons we've learned together. I am proud of the person you continue to evolve into each day. As you embark on new adventures and embrace life's challenges, remember that you are capable of anything you set your mind to. Always remember my love for you knows no bounds.

To my beloved daughter Daisie, now a radiant mother,

As I witness the beauty and grace with which you embrace motherhood, my heart overflows with pride and love. You are gentle, kind, and caring just like you have always been. I am thankful for the joy you bring me and now the joy you give to your daughter. I love you for who you are and cherish each moment we have together. You truly make my world brighter. My love for you will forever be a guiding light through life's journey.

To my cherished daughter Aryanna,
You illuminate me with your laughter, inspire me with your dreams, and fill my heart with pride. Your smile can brighten my darkest days. You are strong, resilient, and the world is waiting for the brilliance only you can bring. As you continue to navigate life's twists and turns with grace and resilience, may you always remember your worth is immeasurable. I cherish and love you beyond words.

To my adored daughter Claire,
My love for you stretches across time and space, wrapping you in warmth, support, and unwavering admiration. Your presence has graced my world with beauty and light. Your courage in the face of adversity inspires me beyond words. As you continue your own unique journey in this life remember to stand tall, embrace your talents, celebrate your successes, and never forget the endless love I have for you.

To my treasured daughter Iilyah Mia Hope, my little engine that could,
You are a precious gift, a beautiful reflection of all that is good in this world. Through life's challenges you have shown tenacity, grace, and unwavering determination. You have a boundless passion for life and your relentless pursuit of dreams serves as a constant reminder of what is possible. You are loved beyond measure, cherished beyond words, and capable of achieving greatness in every step you take. Thank you for showing me what it means to live fearlessly. I love you.

To my courageous younger son Asher,

You light up my life with your endless curiosity. Your bravery to try new things inspires me to keep going. Your laughter fills my soul with unexplainable joy. As I watch you grow and learn I see the world through your eyes, and it brings me such happiness. May you always remember the love of your family and the joy you bring each of us.

To my little valentine Opal,
From the time you entered this world until now you have surpassed the frivolous things I thought I needed in this world. I delight in your cries, your coos, and the sweet smell of you. You inspire me to be the person you need as you grow. May you always have a love of reading and writing just like your Mimmy. Always remember I love you my sweet granddaughter.

To my special duo, Reece and Ryan,
Getting to watch you grow up and into the young men you are becoming has been a blessing in my life. Your interest in my projects is greatly appreciated! Life is going to take you amazing places I just know it. Keep ballin' and remember how much your Aunt Catherine loves you.

To Carter, Amelia, Emory, and Wells,
Stay curious and always remember life is the most valuable classroom. May you always remember how much you are loved by so many.

Special shout out to Aryanna and Claire for the time spent on the beautiful sketches for this book. They are exactly what I dreamed of and more.

Thank you to my mother for always encouraging me to pursue my dreams and for being willing to talk about all things Aunt Ruby with me. You created a desire in me to be a truth speaker and truth sharer. Thank you for being an inspiration to me to chase my dreams.

Thank you to my father who inspires me with his creativity and hard work. I am thankful he spurs me on in my journey of life to reach my goals. I am grateful for the ability to call him day or night knowing he will always be there to listen to my ideas and thoughts. Thank you for your dedication to your work and resilience to see things through. You are an inspiration to me.

Thank you to my sister Elizabeth for letting me keep this project a secret and never wondering why I have been absent from the usual things as of late. I love that we live across the street from each other, and I promise never to keep another secret from her;)

SOURCES

Most information attained was in Ruby's police files received through FOIA request.
Harding University Publications
Hannah Wood Lead Archivist at Brackett Library
Searcy Library/Daily Citizen News articles
True Detective Magazine Article March 1965 Volume 82, Number 6
Article from Scott Bonn, Psychology Today
https://www.psychologytoday.com/us/blog/wicked-deeds/201806/organized-versus-disorganized-serial-predators
Harding Bison article on Botham Jean
at
https://scholarworks.harding.edu/cgi/viewcontent.cgi?article=2990&context=thebison
Websters Dictionary
Some pictures obtained from Sherilyn Eldred
One bit of info from https://aymag.com/most-likely-to-be-murdered/
Clarita Bartley
Jerry V. Bass

www.ingramcontent.com/pod-product-compliance
Lightning Source LLC
Chambersburg PA
CBHW070801280326
41934CB00012B/3001